D0093659

PICK THREE

ALSO BY RANDI ZUCKERBERG

DOT COMPLICATED

DOT.

PICK THREE

YOU CAN HAVE IT ALL
(JUST NOT EVERY DAY)

Randi Zuckerberg

DEY ST.

An Imprint of WILLIAM MORROW

HarperCollins books may be purchased for educational, business, or sales promotional use. For information, please email the Special Markets Department at SPsales@harpercollins.com.

FIRST EDITION

Designed by Renata De Oliveira

Library of Congress Cataloging-in-Publication Data has been applied for.

ISBN 978-0-06-284282-4 (hardcover)

ISBN 978-0-06-284919-9 (international edition)

18 19 20 21 22   LSC   10 9 8 7 6 5 4 3 2 1

BRENT. ASHER. SIMI.
MY PICK THREE
TILL THE END OF TIME.

CONTENTS

PREFACE

I'm honored to witness your blossoming into a happier, more focused, and even more kick-ass version of the amazing person you already are. Pick Three has completely changed my life and I'm so excited to share my methods with you. By giving myself permission to focus on doing a few things well every day, rather than trying to be perfect at everything (and failing miserably) I've been able to redefine what success and happiness look like. I've also unloaded a lot of the guilt I've carried around for years. Now I wake up every morning, look in the mirror, and say, "Work. Sleep. Family. Fitness. Friends. Pick Three." And trust me, it works! But you'll learn more about how it works as you read on. . . .

I'd love to hear your Pick Three. Post on social media with #pickthree or tag me @randizuckerberg and let me know what you've learned about yourself, where your own Pick Three skews (mine's Work, Fitness, and Family right now), and where you'd like to improve. Actions like these help us hold ourselves accountable on our quest for perfect imbalance. Wait, what? Read on. . . .

INTRODUCTION

"I would rather die of passion than of boredom."—VINCENT VAN GOGH

This year I made an oath to myself to stop feeling guilty about everything. Guilty about not being perfect all the time (or ever, really), guilty for not having the most exemplary wardrobe or flawless body, guilty for eating too much gluten or drinking too much coffee, guilty for making investments or taking career risks that don't pan out, guilty for not responding to every e-mail, guilty for not being the perfect mom, wife, or friend. (I'm exhausted just writing about all this unnecessary guilt.)

When I dug deep and thought about why I've wasted so much of my short, precious time on earth apologizing for things, I realized that it stems from an intense pressure to *have it all, do it all,* and *be it all* at the same time. You can't be everything to everyone, whether you're a student, a parent, a boss, an employee, a spouse, an athlete, an artist, a friend in need, an entrepreneur, or a multihyphenate. We're told to be great at everything in order to achieve some lofty and unrealistic level of balance across all areas of our lives.

I'm here to burst that bubble. I think the idea of being well balanced is about as off-kilter as a born-and-bred Scotsman dancing the Irish jig (get it, off *kilt*-er?). I believe that striving to be well balanced is a lousy setup for one of three things: failure, unreasonable expectations, or worse, MEDIOCRITY! *Shudder.*

The people you love, the passions you have, and the things you want to accomplish shouldn't be limited by how well you can balance everything because, let's face it, you can't achieve anything of importance or significance by striving to HAVE IT ALL in a twenty-four-hour period. Talk about stress!

Speaking of having it all, even though I do subscribe to the "more-is-more" philosophy of life, I'm sorry, but "all" is not necessarily better. Have you ever gone to one of those twenty-four-hour all-you-can-eat Vegas buffets? Ten servings later, at 3 A.M., did you still feel that "having it all" was a good life decision?

Whatever it is you want to excel at—whether it's your career, your family, your fitness level, a personal passion, a specific project, your social life, anything!—you have to prioritize it by putting it at the top of your to-do list. Over and over and over and over and over again.

Well balanced? Ha! I have a different theory to success.

LIVING LOPSIDED

The idea of being well lopsided first came into my life when I was applying to college. I was an ambitious, motivated go-getter at the highly competitive Horace Mann High School in Riverdale, New York. Like every other New York prep school student, I thought that the pinnacle of life was getting into Harvard University. Can somebody say PRESSURE!?

The problem was, I wasn't the typical person you think of when you think Harvard. I'd been held back a year in two subjects. I didn't have perfect SAT scores. I wasn't student body president. I hadn't started a nonprofit or interned for some fancy company. I had zero connections or legacy. Instead, I was a theater nerd. Watch out, Ivy League, here I come—with jazz hands!

Growing up I spent every waking moment singing or being involved in the theater, any way I could. Summers were dedicated to touring with a semiprofessional opera company. I performed in multiple shows a year. I created my own independent study where I attended the dress rehearsals of operas at Lincoln Center and wrote term papers based on those works. I took AP music theory instead of calculus. I dropped science my senior year of high school so I could focus more on music. My dream was to perform on Broadway, and if I couldn't perform on Broadway, to help *run* Broadway.

As much as my family supported me and my personal life plans, I'm not really sure anybody believed I'd ever get into Fair Harvard. My mom said she hung her head in embarrassment as Mr. Singer, my high school guidance counselor, asked her which college was my top choice and she had to reveal what she thought was the most implausible choice of all: Harvard. As if I could *actually* be accepted. But, encouraging my dreams, my mom took me to tour the campus, where, of course, I fell in love with the school. From the gorgeous colonial buildings to the traditions and history, I wanted it BAD.

We met with an admissions officer who said something that sticks with me all these years later (well, not *that* many years, geez!). Her words became the foundation for this book: "Randi," said the admissions officer, "Harvard looks for two kinds of people. One, those who are well balanced, and two, those who are well lopsided. The well-balanced students serve as the backbone of the class, but it's the well-lopsided students who make the class incredibly interesting."

Oh my gosh, that's me! I remember thinking. *I'm one of the lopsided ones!* Fast-forward nine months and there I was, receiving a thick Harvard-embossed envelope stuffed with my acceptance letter to the class of 2003! My first encounter with the world of well-lopsidedness was a win! I decided there and then to make it more than just my motto to live life lopsided, but also to pass on the wisdom and knowledge this strategy has afforded me as well.

From the moment I sat in that admissions office as an over-eager, starry-eyed high school junior, I decided to follow my passions, to be one of the *interesting* ones, and to dive into things the best way possible—living the lopsided dream.

As I moved on from higher learning to the real world, I knew I needed something to help ground my many tasks in a way that an app just couldn't do. I had a bevy of outside interests, I was working a high-pressure job, and my husband and I were on our way to having a family. Stress was weighing me down. Right when I thought I'd have to bow to the pressure and give up a few of my favorite things, like staying fit or seeing live theater all the time, I remembered the admissions officer's description of being "well lopsided" and an idea hatched.

I don't have to give up anything! I thought. *Maybe instead of being balanced, I should turn this whole thing on its head and focus on being unbalanced! Instead of trying to do everything every single day, what if I look at the major buckets of my life (work, sleep, family, fitness, friends) and PICK THREE to focus on each day? That way, I can do those three things WELL and I can pick a different three tomorrow. Over time I'll be well rested, fit, successful, and cultured—all with kids in tow!* And thus, from a Harvard admissions meeting, where I wasn't even expected to get in, Pick Three was born.

I'M SURE I'M NOT THE ONLY ONE WHO'S HAD THAT ONE STRESSFUL moment that truly weighs you down. We're all carrying the weight of the world on our shoulders. In fact, if I took a good hard look at the things *you* accomplish each week, I'd probably be asking you to autograph this book for *me*! When you think of all the things we attempt to balance, it can feel completely overwhelming.

Here's a rough list of things I would have to do every day in order to **have it all:**

- Raise two boys to be good men who work hard and treat women with respect
- Spend meaningful time with my husband
- Run my business well and keep everyone happy (not easy in New York!)
- Write a book (aka this book)
- Prep and host my weekly SiriusXM radio show
- Eat healthy (except during Pumpkin Spice Latte season, but liquids don't count as food, right?)
- Plan my travel for the forty-plus speeches and lectures I do each year

- Coordinate childcare for when I am on the road
- Feel guilty about traveling and not being with my children
- Maintain our home (except that I sort of live at the airport . . .)
- Keep in touch with family (sorry for not calling, Mom! What time zone is it again?)
- Fulfill board of directors and advisory board obligations
- See sixty-plus Broadway and Off-Broadway shows a year for Tony Awards and Chita Rivera Awards voting
- Post to social media accounts
- Check other people's social media accounts (and consequently decide their lives are so much better than mine)
- Respond to an avalanche of e-mails and messages (why does that little number on my inbox never go down?!?!)
- Tell myself, "Randi, you should really respond to that e-mail," while knowing full well that as soon as a few more e-mails come in above it, it will vanish from my mind forever

Oh! I can't forget my aspirational goals:

- See my friends. Ever.
- Stay in shape (ha!)
- Sleep (capital HA!)
- Shower (Don't judge.)

Well, that was exhausting. Maybe I should just crawl back into bed and call it a day.

What if I reframed that overwhelming list from Things to Do Today to Things to Do *This Year*? Or over three years? Or ten! This way, I could choose a few things to do each day and do those few things really, really well, completely focused on the tasks I choose and not so much on EVERYTHING ALL AT ONCE. (caps lock underline UGH!)

Even with so much on my plate, I consider myself to be one of the extremely lucky ones. I have a wonderful, loving partner in my husband, Brent, who takes on a huge amount of parenting and household work. I have an incredible team at Zuckerberg Media who make sure everything runs smoothly. And I work with amazing partners at Jim Henson Productions, Universal Kids, CAA, HarperCollins, and SiriusXM. I have the monetary resources to hire trustworthy childcare. And I have loving, supportive friends and family. Plus, as one friend said recently, "You're only as happy as your least happy child," and both of my kids are healthy and happy, thank God.

The truth is, most of the time we're all thinking about how happy or unhappy we are. Are we happier playing with the kids at home? Happier running away to the gym for an hour? Or happier sitting at work finalizing the last paragraph of that report? Happiness is something we naturally strive for in life. But with the stress of finding *balance,* it's no wonder we're all so darn unhappy.

The 2007 World Happiness Report had the United States ranked third-happiest among the thirty-five countries in the Organization for Economic Co-operation and Development. But before you start celebrating, less than ten years later, in 2016, the

U.S. dropped to nineteenth out of thirty-five. Reasons for this drop include declining social support and increased government corruption (no comment).[1]

To further the unhappiness, all you have to do is spend *one second* on your favorite social media platform, and suddenly you're bombarded with images of everyone else's perfect lives, their fancy vacations, their intellectual book clubs, leaving you feeling that everyone else has got it down WAY better than you. You start to think that maybe you're not the #ninja you thought you were five minutes ago. Of course, deep down we know that everyone is just putting on a show online, broadcasting only the very best, glossiest parts of their lives—but we still can't help but feel a bit inadequate. Sound familiar?

In 2016, the Pitt's Center for Research in Media surveyed 1,787 young adults nationwide about their use of eleven popular social media platforms (Instagram, Facebook, etc.). The people who reported using the most platforms (seven to eleven) had more than *three times* the risk of depression and anxiety than people who used the fewest (zero to two platforms). Maintaining a regular presence across many sites (aka social media multitasking) led to poorer attention, cognition, and mood.[2]

Along with that, a Royal Society for Public Health study reports that social media brought out anxiety, fear of missing out (FOMO), bullying, high levels of depression, and low levels of sleep quality among teens.[3] And to top it all off, a 2017 You.gov poll found that 26 percent of Americans say receiving a negative comment on social media has ruined their day.[4] Even worse—it might not even be a human who left the bad comment! With messaging bots on the rise, it could be a robot that winds up making or breaking your day.

FOMO, depression, social media comparisons—you get it, and I'm right there with you. But you're not here for all this doom and gloom. As I'm writing this book I'm in a place where I feel truly, deeply happy—take that, U.S. happiness rate! In many ways, I already have it all. All the #Blessed hashtags combined.

But it wasn't always this way, nor is it always this way. Things go differently than planned. Emergencies—big and little—pop up at the most unexpected and inconvenient times. In true neurotic Jewish mom form, I always worry that the better things are, the sooner the other stiletto will drop. I fear that glass half full is going to spill any minute.

We all have different situations and challenges. Some of us raise children as single parents or work multiple, grueling jobs to achieve financial independence. Many maneuver through the difficult hands life has dealt. In other words, many of you are IRL #SUPERHEROES. Not from the pages of DC Comics, but in reality, you're making the world turn for those you love and care about, no matter the cost.

Whatever situation we find ourselves in, there is one common denominator: we all feel incredible pressure to balance everything we need, have, and want, and to get it perfectly right—*or else*.

But what if we didn't have that pressure weighing on our shoulders all the time? What if it were okay to pick a *few* things to focus on each day? What if it were all right to give yourself permission to be well lopsided instead of well balanced? And what if I showed you a way that focusing on just a few things at a time could actually make you *happier* in the long run (as long as you eventually choose everything on your to-do list at some point)? Would you sign up? Well, get your cursive skills ready (my what?), because I'm going to show you how it's done!

WORK. SLEEP. FAMILY. FITNESS. FRIENDS. PICK THREE.

When people hear that I'm on the road for work roughly one hundred days a year, their most common response is one of horror. "Don't you miss your children?" Of course I miss my children! I'm not a monster. But I also love what I do. There's nothing I enjoy more than meeting fellow entrepreneurs, students, and dreamers creating and innovating new ideas from around the world. The feeling I get when I travel for work, sharing stories, making new friendships, and inspiring others is my bona fide Happy Place. But if I were focused on being well balanced all the time, I wouldn't be on the road nearly as much as I am.

Providing for my family is extremely important to me and contributes to my own sense of purpose and meaning. So sure, I'd probably be, like, a 3 percent better mom if I were traveling less—but I'd also be a lot less happy. I have tremendous passion and enormous pride in my work. If I dialed that back, I'd be dialing back what's at the very core of my identity and sense of self. To satisfy the imbalance of what makes us happiest, we have to make trade-offs in different areas of our lives.

My kids know how much I adore them. I've carved out a life for myself that allows me to do the work I love, then come home and give quality, undivided attention to the people I care about. I know a group of fantastic moms from my sons' school who look out for my boys and send messages and photos to keep me in the loop of what's happening while I'm away. Do I beat myself up that I'm gone so much? Absolutely. I'm in Round 4,245,003 of my own personal title fight. But I feel like I've got guilt up against the ropes, because I've made a commitment to stop feeling bad about not having the ideal work-life balance, *because it's impossible!* Now I know that it's only when I give myself permission to be lopsided toward work on some days and lopsided toward my family on other days that I actually do the best job at both.

When I look back at the past twenty years of my life, all my proudest, most rewarding, greatest moments—the moments I will hopefully live to tell my great-grandchildren about—all happened when I allowed myself to be lopsided. Had I chosen to be well balanced I wouldn't be where I am today—where I'm HAPPY to be today. Thank heavens for living at a sloped angle!

For me, half the fun of being lopsided is being able to throw myself headfirst into things that excite me. Whether it's work, sleep, family, fitness, or friends, I can't ever know exactly what's going to happen, but when I'm armed with equal parts passion and data, I always know I'll be glad I tried. Living life loudly and lopsidedly on your own terms, without guilt, without caring what other people think or say, without allowing yourself to be frozen from a fear of failing, is where the fun really begins.

There are so many ways to be a well-lopsided person. Some are conscious choices. Some are forced due to situations beyond your control. Some accommodate the interests of loved ones.

Some are decisions about what NOT to make a priority rather than what to focus on. All of these choices are just as valid and wonderful and appreciated as the next. There is no right or wrong way to be lopsided, as long as you aren't so lopsided that it affects your health and happiness, or hurts the people who love you—although sometimes that's exactly what happens (we'll discuss this later on).

In this book I'm going to share interviews I conducted with some of the most well-lopsided people I know. Like Arianna Huffington, who, after suffering a health wake-up call of her own, shifted her entire focus to the importance of sleep awareness for professionals. Or Dr. Adam Griesemer, who often works forty-hour-plus shifts as a pediatric organ transplant surgeon. I spoke with Melinda Arons, who left a lucrative role at Facebook to go all-in on Hillary Clinton's presidential campaign. I chatted with Rebecca Soffer, who lost both her parents in a short time and channeled her pain into helping others who are grieving after the death of a loved one. I talked to Brad Takei, who decided to make it his life's purpose to help his husband, George Takei, succeed in all he does. And I sat down with Reshma Saujani, who realized that losing two political elections was key to understanding her life's purpose.

I'm going to share stories of others who became lopsided in different ways—some by choice, some by situation. I'm going to arm you with all my tips, tricks, and life hacks to becoming your absolute best, well-lopsided self. At the back of this book is a workbook for you to track your own Pick Three progress and help hold yourself accountable.

Your journey in how to better prioritize, focus, and, yes, surrender, started the minute you opened this book. I applaud you for choosing an alternative path to happiness. See? You're doing great at this lopsided thing already!

Pick Three is my motto, my creed, my personal life force, and I'm honored to share it with you.

Screw balance. Let's be interesting! Let's be different!

PICK THREE

1

WHAT IS
PICK THREE?

LET'S GET LOPSIDED!

"There is no such thing as a work-life balance. Everything worth fighting for unbalances your life."

—ALAIN DE BOTTON

The first time I actually said "Pick Three" out loud was in a moment of frustration. It was approximately the one hundredth time I was part of a conference panel where I'd been asked by the moderator, "Randi, you're a mom AND you have a career. How do you balance it all?" Of course, nobody would ever ask the *men* on the panel that question. Like it's some ancient secret that the exact same skill set that makes someone a great parent (organization, prioritization, long-term planning, patience, creativity) also makes someone just as great an employee or entrepreneur (shocker!).

Most of the time when I'd get that same inquiry (that is, every time I'm on a panel), I'd grit my teeth, force a smile, and say something trite about how I try to balance it all. Except for one day when I just couldn't muster up the strength to BS through it anymore. After the unsuspecting moderator asked how I balance it all, I shook my head and said, "I don't.

"In order to set myself up for success, I know I can only realistically do *three* things well every day. So, every day when I wake up, I think to myself: Work. Sleep. Family. Friends. Fitness. Pick Three. I can pick a different three tomorrow, and a different three the following day. But today, I can only pick three. As long as I wind up picking everything over the long run, then I'm balancing my imbalance. It's solving the great entrepreneur's dilemma."

And almost immediately I was quoted in business publications around the world. Pick Three had gone viral.

I later realized that the dilemma doesn't just apply to entrepreneurs—it applies to EVERYONE. No matter what you do for a living, where you live, or what your responsibilities are, nobody can have it all without a little bit of sacrifice, focus, and energy. Over time I stopped calling it "the Entrepreneur's Dilemma" and renamed it as Pick Three. Not only is it more inclusive, *it's instructional*.

The five main categories in your life might be slightly different than mine, but for the purposes of this book—and the forthcoming exercises—let's assume that my five categories work for you as well.

WORK, SLEEP, FAMILY, FITNESS, FRIENDS: THE BREAKDOWN

Work

Projects where you contribute time and, in return, derive value, which could be in the form of money, passion, meaning, a sense of contribution to something greater, or a stepping-stone to a long-term goal. Value could result from a traditional job, a passion project, a class or coursework at school, an internship, a charitable initiative, etc. You are creating output for some sort of input.

Sleep

That pesky thing that eats up 30 percent of your day (if you're lucky!).

Family

This could be the family you were born into, the family you create, the family you choose. This doesn't have to mean your biological family, either. Maybe your church is your family. Maybe you have a "modern" family, or a nontraditional family. However you define family in your life, this is the category for prioritizing it.

Fitness

While the term fitness conjures up images of dumbbells and sweat, to me, this category reflects a broader goal of self-care and health: physical fitness, mental fitness, emotional well-being, mindfulness, stress management, and healthy eating.

Friends

This is my personal catch-all for things that are fun. When you think about friends, you typically think about the closest people in your life. But this is where I also think about side hobbies and outside interests—the people and activities that bring pleasure outside of work and family.

Now that we have our five categories down, it's time for the fun part.

PICK THREE

Now is the time for ruthless prioritization. So, sorry, you don't get to pick all five. Not today. Not any day. If you want to be great at what you do, Pick Three and only three. And don't waste one minute feeling guilty or bad about the two you didn't pick. Because you'll get another chance to pick them tomorrow. Or the day after. Or next month—it will happen.

Because every single day you get to pick a new three of these categories to focus on, you can pick the same three as the day before, or switch gears and pick a different three. It's YOUR CHOICE. Maybe you have a weekday Pick Three and a weekend Pick Three. Maybe you have a summer Pick Three and a winter Pick Three. Maybe it changes every day. Regardless, Pick Three enables you to have the best in terms of short-term focus and long-term balance.

I can hear you now: *"Randi, I can totally pick all five! I can exercise with my friends and call my mom on the way to work! Fitness, Friends, and Family, done! Two to go!"*

While I have no doubt that every once in a while, for a day or two, you can manage to hit all five of these, it's really not sustainable in the long run. If you try to accomplish all five things WELL (keyword: *well*), you're headed for complete and utter burnout. You're not going to grand-slam all five at a high-functioning level. Sure, it's humanly possible to touch upon your family, your friends, your work, your sleep, and your fitness every day. But doing all five things—even just for a day—means you're probably not doing any of them with any real depth.

We've been taught that *imbalance* is a dirty word, but I think it's actually the key to success and happiness. The Pick Three lifestyle can help you nail life (and keep your sanity) by being well lopsided. When you focus solely on the trio you choose each day, prioritizing becomes totally manageable and you give yourself the permission to do those three things with the kind of excellence that will propel you further than weeks of half-assed focus. Over time, as you pick a different three every day, it evens out into—*abracadabra!*—BALANCE!! Okay, so it's not magic, but how great would it be to reach the end of the day and know that you not only accomplished all three things you set out to do, but you did a fantastic job at each of them, too?!

Norwegians have known this for years. According to the World Happiness Report (yes, that thing again), Norway has jumped from fourth place in 2016 to first place in 2017, followed by Denmark and Iceland.

Why Nordic countries, you ask? Isn't it freezing there? Heck, yeah, it is, but weather plays little into happiness. What those three countries have in common are high values in six key variables: income (work), high life expectancy (fitness), family values (yup), freedom (sleep), trust (friends), and generosity (all of the above).

THE PICK THREE METHOD

THERE ARE A FEW BASIC RULES TO REMEMBER WHEN FOLLOWING THE PICK THREE METHOD:

1. **YOU ONLY GET THREE.** While it's incredibly tempting to try for more (we're an increasingly multitasking culture, after all), remember that we're going for quality over quantity here. Work. Sleep. Family. Friends. Fitness. Pick Three.

2. **BUT HAVE NO FEAR, YOU CAN PICK A DIFFERENT THREE TOMORROW!** No need for buyer's remorse. The beauty of Pick Three is that when you wake up, it's a brand-new day and a brand-new opportunity for you to pick a different three categories to focus on.

3. **NO GUILT!** Keep reminding yourself that you can't do everything well all the time. Give yourself permission to be great at the three things you've picked and try not to waste one precious second feeling guilty about the things you didn't pick. If that's not possible, blame me. After all, I'm the one who told you that you could only pick three things!

4. **BE GREAT!** There's no point to Pick Three if you're not going to go all in on the three things you've picked to focus on. So pick your three and do as amazing a job as you possibly can.

5. **TRACK YOUR CHOICES.** Like any system that holds you accountable, Pick Three works best if you jot down your choices each day and refer back to make sure you are roughly picking all five categories the same amount over the course of time. Whether you want to track it on paper, on your phone, or in our Pick Three app, logging your three daily choices will give you a sense of the broader overall picture of your life—and where you may need to shift a bit more effort.

A SLICE FROM MY OWN PICK THREE PIE

Take a look at my sample week from my own Pick Three journal and think about how you might want to pick and schedule your Pick Three.

MONDAY, SEPTEMBER 4:

To Do: Family. Sleep. Fitness.

Today is Labor Day, which means no one will be shocked, angry, or disappointed if they don't get a response from me. My kids haven't started the school year yet, and my in-laws are in town. I pick Family so I can spend quality time with my kids, husband, and visiting relatives; Sleep since my wonderful, gorgeous, looking-younger-every-day in-laws have volunteered to get up early with the kids (hello, sleeping in!!), and Fitness because my husband and I are going to go on a jog around the park (after sleeping in, that is!).

Ta-da! Pick Three complete!

TUESDAY, SEPTEMBER 5:

To Do: Work. Friends. Family.

I start off the morning with an early-morning television appearance discussing new back-to-school apps and gadgets. I always love hosting segments, but to get TV-ready means I won't be picking Sleep, since I have to wake up at the crack of dawn. My good friend Erica joins me in the studio and we catch up over coffee afterward. Friend time: Check! After that, I head to the office, where I have tons of work to catch up on. That's Work times two! I make it home in time to kiss my boys, help my six-year-old son prep for his first day of school, and catch up with my husband when he gets home from work.

Ta-da: Pick Three crushed!

WEDNESDAY, SEPTEMBER 6:

To Do: Family. Work. Fitness.

At 7 A.M., I put my six-year-old on the bus for his very first day of first grade. Which means Sleep is out (but I wouldn't miss this for anything). On Wednesdays, I spend the day at SiriusXM, hosting my radio show *Dot Complicated with Randi Zuckerberg,* on Channel 111 Business Radio (shameless plug), so I head straight to the studio to prep for the show, greet my guests, and go on air. Later that evening, I'm heading on a flight to Boston for a work event, so I come home after my radio show ends in order to pack, get in a quick workout (120 burpees! Eek!), and spend some quality time with my boys (playing Pokémon Go), before heading to the airport.

Ta-da: Pick Three next level!

THURSDAY, SEPTEMBER 7:

To Do: Work. Family. Sleep.

I wake up *super* early in Boston to get ready for a big day ahead (where are my in-laws now?). I'm giving a keynote speech to more than a thousand business professionals and entrepreneurs about disruptive tech, social media, and leadership in the digital age, and I need to wake up early to prepare. The speech goes fantastically well (phew), and I follow it up by signing copies of my first book, *Dot Complicated* (another shameless plug!). Then it's off to the airport to head home. I am absolutely exhausted when I get home, but it's just in time to take my sons out for our promised dinner date. Afterward I tuck them into bed and collapse into my own.

Ta-da: Pick Thrzzzzzzz . . .

FRIDAY, SEPTEMBER 8:

To Do: Work. Friends. Family.

YUUUGE day of work. Whenever I'm on a business trip, there's always a double-plus pile to do when I return, and today is no different. I have SIX hours of back-to-back meetings. But it's Friday, so no matter what, if I'm in town I always make sure to be home in time for Shabbat dinner with my family. Shabbat in our home is really special. We light candles, we say a prayer of gratitude, and we each go around the table recounting the many things we've been thankful for during the week. We do a special "yum yum" blessing, too, because on Shabbat, we get to eat dessert before dinner! Talk about something to look forward to! (Note to self: Why is there no *dessert* option for Pick Three?) Once the boys are in bed and our babysitter arrives, my husband and I go to an Off-Broadway show and meet up with some old friends. When the show finishes, we all know we should go home and get some sleep, but we go out to a jazz bar to have a nightcap instead. *It's 1 A.M. already?! Good thing I didn't pick Sleep.*

Ta-da: Pick Three complete!

SATURDAY, SEPTEMBER 9:

To Do: Family. Fitness. Work.

It's another gorgeous day in NYC, so we use one of our favorite life hacks to get in a longer run with our sons in tow: Scooters! Even if we have to occasionally pull the boys uphill, it's a double Fitness/Family Pick Three bonus! We decide we've earned a delicious brunch (with the rest of the unofficial religious zealots of NYC, aka *Brunchtarians*) before I'm off to work finishing deadlines on this book. I head inside for the rest of the day to enjoy the beautiful warming glow of my computer screen.

Ta-da: Pick Three slaughtered.

SUNDAY, SEPTEMBER 10:

To Do: Sleep. Family. Friends.

Sunday = Funday! My husband offers to get up early with the boys, so I get to sleep in. Woot! On Sunday evenings, we grill outside, so we have some friends and their kids over to join. I'm heading out for another business trip tomorrow, so I call it an early night so I can hit the ground running tomorrow.

Ta-da: Pick Three, mic drop.

HOW DID I DO? LET'S TALLY UP THE RESULTS:

    WORK: 5

    SLEEP: 3

    FAMILY: 7

    FRIENDS: 3

    FITNESS: 3

I'm glad I was so lopsided in favor of my family this week, because I'll be heading out on a four-day business trip next week, which means I'll really only get to spend time with my children and husband the next weekend. My coming week will be very lopsided in the direction of work, so when I return I could stand to prioritize sleep, friends, and fitness a bit more—especially since I won't be able to do that much of any of those while I'm away on business. Overall I don't have heavy guilt or pressure weighing me down, so I feel pretty great about my choices. I'm able to close the chapter on the past week feeling successful, complete, and, most of all, happy.

By using the Pick Three mantra, I'm able to eliminate any self-condemnation or shame I might have from a generic, all-over-the-place to-do list. I promise, you will feel the same. Pick Three leaves you better able to focus, prioritize, and carry out actions in the areas you choose. And at the end of the week you'll be able to take a mental snapshot of where you spent most of your time and energy, where being the most lopsided served you, and take stock of anything you'd like to change or adjust in the coming days.

If you know that you're going to be incredibly lopsided in

certain categories in future days or weeks, try to choose the other categories now, before life gets too out of whack and you end up sleeping all day long or working until you can't see straight. There's well lopsided and then there's *Help! I've fallen and I can't get up* lopsided, and we don't want to go there.

To get an idea of how Pick Three works, I wanted to lay out a few examples of others living by the Pick Three mantra, proof that it works the best when you make intentional choices every single day.

EMMY

Emmy is basically most of us *before* taking on the Pick Three lifestyle. She tries to be too balanced by picking everything and ultimately spreads herself too thin. She picks three things a day but often tries to squeeze in a fourth as well. After a week she feels stressed out, run down, and exhausted. Here's a slice from her Pick Three journal:

"Monday: Work, Family, Fitness. Oh, and Sleep! I overslept my alarm and went to a later spin class than usual. I rushed out there and was making good time, but then there was a ton of traffic so I was super late to work, which meant I had to stay later than I had planned, which meant tonight's special family dinner was not-so-special takeout. They forgot to put in my son's burrito, so I ended up having to drive back to the restaurant. When I got home the kids were starving and cranky, so I let them spend the evening watching TV while I caught up on e-mails. Maybe tomorrow will be better."

Can you tell what went wrong with Emmy's day? That's right, she picked *four*—Fitness, Work, Family, *and* Sleep—and consequently everything went awry. Had she stuck with three choices for the day, she wouldn't have been late to work, she would have enjoyed her spin class, and she would've been home earlier to spend quality time with her family like she'd hoped. Instead, her multitasking kept her from accomplishing any of her goals.

STEVE

Steve is the person who's a bit TOO lopsided. He overprioritizes work so much that he often focuses on only two choices from his Pick Three—which leads to unhealthy consequences. Here's a look at Steve's Pick Three journey.

"Thursday: Work, Sleep, Friends. I have a huge work project coming up, so I've chosen Work as one of my Pick Three every single day for the past two weeks. Maybe tonight I'll try to get to bed at 1 A.M. and sleep in until 6:45 instead of 6:30 tomorrow. Probably not, though—I'm so stressed, I can never fall or stay asleep. I told Tyrone I'd meet up with him for drinks later, but this project has me chained to the computer. I've been eating my takeout lunches and dinners in front of my screen since last Saturday. I feel like I've put on ten pounds! When this project finishes I'm going to pick Fitness every day! I hate how I feel."

Right off the bat we can tell how overworked Steve is. He's tired, irritable, making bad food choices, and suffering the consequences. He's really only chosen Work to focus on, skipping out on his friend and sleeping less than five hours a night, if that. A lack of rest and stress plus unhealthy eating has left Steve depleted. He wants to choose Fitness, but is not making the time for it. Now he's feeling the effects of being too lopsided in one direction. Steve needs to summon his willpower to focus on his own health outside of work, otherwise things will quickly go from bad to worse.

JAMES

James is like the Pick Three Goldilocks—he's got his well-lopsidedness down just right. Here's a day in the life of James:

"Sunday: Sleep, Fitness, Friends. One more day of the weekend left! I sleep in until ten, feeling reenergized. I take a twenty-five-mile ride with my bike group and catch up with a few riders over brunch at the end. After the long day, I shower and read, taking my time doing both. In the evening I enjoy a quiet evening with Netflix and a glass of wine, preparing myself for a busy week ahead. I know I'll be choosing Work every day this week, so I'm glad I had such a long ride today, as Fitness will have to fall by the wayside until Saturday. Until then, I'll make sure to get plenty of rest to keep the stress at bay."

James has got Pick Three down! He knows he's going to choose Work for a few days, so he factors the loss of Fitness into his current schedule, giving himself permission to be lopsided for a short amount of time. He knows how important choosing Sleep is to his stress levels, so he makes it a priority, while combining Friends and Fitness to ensure both goals are complete. Well done, James! He's a Pick Three superstar!

YOU CAN SEE HOW PICK THREE WORKS (AND DOESN'T WORK) FOR such a wide variety of people. Some people have flexible jobs and can truly pick a different three things every day. Some may find it easier to have a regular routine during the week and then a different Pick Three on the weekends. It's hard to get the perfect mix, but with practice and your very own journal, you can crush it at picking three and finding happiness through lopsidedness.

PICK THREE WORKSHOPPING

Ask yourself:

Which Pick Three have you chosen today? How about yesterday? Tomorrow?

Which Pick Three would you like to be focusing on instead of what you are currently focused on?

Which Pick Three were you focused on when you had your proudest accomplishments?

Is there any category you've neglected (or sacrificed) too much? If so, do you constantly feel guilty and beat yourself up?

Does this sound familiar? *If only I had more money, or more time, then I'd be able to focus on my dreams.* How can you put that aside and start working toward them today?

Has there been a day where you were so lopsided you were barely even able to pick two?

Journal your answers to discover how, why, and where your lopsidedness is leaning.

We will have moments when we're able to choose what we want to be lopsided in. Other times our decisions will be made for us by events outside of our control: age, career stage, financial independence, geography, cultural and religious influences, health, education, family pressures—these all play a role.

In many of the books I've read that tout the perfect work-life balance, the author often seems to set their reader up for failure by assuming everyone enjoys the same level of privilege as they do. I'm not going to assume that. I know some people are born lucky; they get to pick their passion with the wind at their back. They have loving, supportive families and the means and resources to pursue their dreams, all while living in good mental and physical health. For others, the day-to-day battle is more of a struggle than an achievement. Just keeping our heads above water deserves its own medal. Sometimes we have to reduce the quest for balance to a simple hashtag on Instagram—which, honestly, feels good enough sometimes. But it doesn't have to be. We can be *better!*

That's why it's not enough to just throw out five categories, tell you to pick three of them, and call it a day. I also want to address the types of situations and circumstances that could lead to your lopsidedness, and how to ensure you put yourself on a path most destined for happiness—no matter which road takes you there.

WITH THAT, PLEASE MEET MY PICK THREE FRIENDS:

THE PASSIONISTA: The person who chooses what they want to be lopsided in for themselves. They are currently in a healthy place where they have the support of a loving family, friends, or community to help make their decision.

THE ELIMINATOR: Sometimes, knowing what NOT to do can help you choose what to pick. Some people have a better sense of what they don't want to focus on, rather than what they do, and they wind up being lopsided more by process of elimination than anything else.

THE SUPERHERO: A person who never actually wanted to be lopsided but, due to unforeseen circumstances (e.g., current events, illness, finances), they were suddenly forced to live life askew.

THE RENOVATOR: Someone who started off as the Passionista but hit a serious roadblock. They've had to rebuild and pivot to reach their goal.

THE MONETIZER: This person capitalizes on one of our basic human needs for Work, Sleep, Family, Fitness, and Friends. Through their products or services, they help us reach our goal that much quicker and achieve more in that area than was originally thought possible.

THE EXPERT: The go-to person who knows a boatload more than I do about why Work, Sleep, Family, Fitness, and Friends are so important in our life.

Which one are you?

I'm sure you can relate to aspects of many of these personas (like when you read the astrology for an Aries but you're a Capricorn, yet the horoscope still makes sense). On any given day your Pick Three might feel very different. But remember, there is no right or wrong way to be lopsided. Whether it's by choice or by circumstance, Pick Three enables you to get through any challenge life throws your way, through carefully chosen focus.

Speaking of challenge, living lopsided does require sacrifice—but the good kind! You have to surrender the notion that you'll be able to accomplish everything, every day. You have to be willing to say, "Bye-bye, gym, not today" or "I'm taking that trip without my family" or "Guess I'll have to survive on four hours of sleep tonight" or "Not answering e-mail today." It's simply not possible to pick Work, Sleep, Family, Fitness, and Friends all at the same time AND to do them well.

It can be difficult feeling like you're giving something up or accepting the fact that you're a mere mortal. But I swear that once you start focusing, prioritizing, and picking three—once you give yourself permission to be well lopsided rather than well balanced—I know you'll find yourself happier, more fulfilled, and way more successful at the things you choose. It's completely changed my life, and I couldn't be more excited for Pick Three to change yours!

2

The Big Five

WORK. SLEEP. FAMILY. FITNESS. FRIENDS. #GOTIME

Work

> *"The typical office worker spends forty to sixty hours per week at their desk—that's a lot of time! It's so important to find a job that fits your life."*
>
> —MARYJO FITZGERALD,
> ECONOMIC COMMUNICATIONS MANAGER OF GLASSDOOR

I'm not going to lie: sitting down to write this chapter felt a bit like going to therapy. If I had to pinpoint the one problem area of my own Pick Three, it's that I always want to pick Work. If I'm not crazy busy working on something, or circling the globe for speaking engagements, I somehow find a way to invent new projects. I actively have to tell myself to pick Work *less* and focus on the other areas of my life a bit more. Especially as a mom, I feel pretty guilty saying that out loud.

What drives people like me to constantly seek out intense work environments? Why do some of us choose to repeatedly be so lopsided toward our careers? Certainly there are many people out there for whom work is just a paycheck. Some people derive meaning from relationships and activities outside of their careers.

So why do some of us put so much meaning on what we do professionally, making our work such a critical part of our identity? And what happens when we dial it back? What effect would it have if we stopped picking Work altogether? And what happens when we shift our priorities, or when life hits us with something that forces us to pick Work a little bit more or a little bit less? Getting to the core of these questions is critical to understanding the role that work plays in each of our individual Pick Three goals—and, truth be told, for my own sanity as well.

I've always felt that the key to success is hard work. There's simply no shortcut in life to putting in the hours, hunkering down, and working your butt off. Whenever I see someone else being successful and I wish it were me, it simply makes me hungrier, and I work even harder.

But this isn't a recent development. Ever since I can remember, I've been a hard worker. From the day I could say the word *Harvard,* I wanted to go there. Which meant working and studying all throughout middle school and high school. My parents provided a wonderful, comfortable upbringing, and they paid for my education so I never had crippling student loan debt. Yet I always had a little nagging voice in the back of my head saying, *Randi, you can't depend on anyone else in this life. Work hard. Earn things for yourself. Make your own money.*

Whether it was helping my dad in his dental office after I finished my homework, caddying at the local bridge club, or babysitting my younger siblings and their friends for five dollars an hour (there's monetary value in being the oldest of four children), I never turned down an opportunity to work.

And it wasn't enough for me to just work. I wanted my money to work, too. I didn't have much to my name, so I enlisted my dad to help me understand the stock market so I could start investing. I ultimately chose three stocks: McDonald's (because it was delicious and I liked to go there on special occasions), American Express (because my parents had a card and used it to buy me cool things) and, only because it had a cool name, I chose this new stock called "Google." Guess which one did the best?

Throughout high school, I worked as a restaurant hostess at the Central Square Café in Westchester, New York. I tutored local students (once I was accepted to Harvard I was able to triple my prices!), and I got promoted to head caddy at the bridge club, which meant, in addition to a bump in salary, I now got to manage other caddies. Hello, upper management!

In college, when everyone else was backpacking through Europe, I was working, often taking on two or three internships at the same time, all while continuing my private tutoring business. I even turned down an opportunity to perform at the world-famous Edinburgh Fringe Festival in order to take on a summer job. I'll admit that one was a tough decision.

I didn't even take any time between college and entering the workforce! I had dreams of hanging out with friends, traveling, enjoying New York City. But no. A long weekend was what I got. I graduated from Harvard on a Thursday and began working in New York at Ogilvy & Mather the following Monday. At Ogilvy, I regularly worked twelve-hour-plus days, but never thought twice about it because all my friends across every industry I knew of were doing the same. When you're in your early twenties, you're still very much in the "building" phase of your career, and if you have ambitious career goals, being lopsided toward Work is more of an expectation than a choice.

Back then I still had the energy to go out with my friends until all hours of the night—*every night*. We were living in the city that never sleeps and wanted to take full advantage of it. When I first began dating my husband, we were both twenty-two, and I remember having the philosophy that if we came home before 4 A.M., it was officially a "lame" evening. Somewhere along the years, that was revised to 2 A.M. Then midnight. Now, when we're lying in bed at 10 P.M., we often remind ourselves of that too-cool time limit and laugh.

I thought I was working hard living in New York City, but you haven't seen anything about what being work-lopsided looks like until you've worked at an early-stage tech start-up! Moving out to Silicon Valley to work at Facebook in 2005 redefined what intense work meant for me.

Back then Facebook was only a few dozen employees in a small office above a Chinese restaurant. Everyone did everything. If you didn't know how to do something, you figured it out and did it anyway. At a start-up, the pace, the hours, the atmosphere are all so intense. Your work becomes your life. There is no separation. No balance. Colleagues become your best friends, your family, your *everything*. It all melds together. Which means you're pretty much working all the time, which is a huge reason start-ups are often dominated by young people without families of their own yet. You essentially have to pick Work as all three of your Pick Three just to survive.

Stay with me and try not to be too shocked when I tell you what we did for fun: we worked MORE. Every few months, we'd hold a hackathon for the employees. Everyone would be invited to pull an all-nighter at the office and work on a project for twelve straight hours (what sort of invite is that!?). The catch—or the fun part, rather—was that the project you worked on couldn't be at all related to your day job. You couldn't sit in a corner and get your work e-mail down to inbox zero. You couldn't work on a presentation for an upcoming meeting. This was twelve straight hours of passion project completion, anything new and creative. If you were still standing at seven the next morning, you got to present your idea to everyone in the company, followed by a pancake breakfast.

I know what you're thinking, and you're right. Our idea of a break from working was to *work on other things??* Yes, this is why start-up entrepreneurs are crazy! It's in our DNA to work, work, work, and never rest. How often is Elon Musk coming up with some new way to get to the moon, speed across the country, never pay for gas? The Boring Company? Elon Musk is anything but boring! Relaxing for even one moment gives your competitors the chance to catch up, which can mean the end of your business. So yes, we worked for work. And, we also worked for fun. I don't want to scare you, but if you're reading this book, thinking of starting your own company, and don't have this worker mentality, you might want to think twice. Work to entrepreneurs is fun, and our Facebook hackathons were fun incarnate.

I don't want to brag or anything, but I have two hackathon projects that I'm particularly proud of. The first was an employee eighties cover band called Feedbomb. Made up of current and former Facebook employees, Feedbomb played at company parties, charity events, you name it. Our motto was: We play for free, and you get what you pay for. We may not have been the world's greatest rock band, but we had a lot of heart (and we played Heart songs as well!).

My second hackathon idea, and the one I'm most proud of, wound up being rolled out to two *BILLION* people. In fact, it's probably on your phone right now. You may have even used it! It's called Facebook Live.

I was (and still am) super passionate about the intersection between digital content and digital media. Back in 2010, when we weren't watching *Game of Thrones* on demand from our laptops, when Netflix and Amazon weren't spending billions of dollars on original, beautifully produced series, I spent a lot of time wondering if there could be a world in which television networks could live *inside* of Facebook. I started envisioning a place where anyone, not just giant TV conglomerates, could speak directly to their audience whenever they wanted to using Facebook as their medium of delivery. Since nothing like this existed, I went directly to some of the big networks I had led successful partnerships with previously—companies like CNN and ABC News—but since the concept was so new, I had trouble explaining my vision in a way that they could buy into, so I got turned down. Everywhere. But I didn't give up on the vision, I just had to do it myself. So at the very next hackathon, I created "Facebook Live with Randi Zuckerberg."

It was a flop. Only two people watched my first broadcast: Karen and Edward Zuckerberg. My parents.

I was so dejected, I didn't even stay up the full twelve hours to present my vision to the company. I gave up, went home, and went to bed.

But somewhere something struck a chord, because only a few weeks later I got a phone call from pop star Katy Perry's manager saying that Katy wanted to use my Facebook Live show to launch her world tour. As I was about to downplay my creation—*"Sorry, but it's not a real television show, it was just a little project I hacked together"*—I stopped myself and asked, *Randi, what would your male colleagues do?* They'd want to meet Katy Perry. They would MAKE. IT. WORK.

And so, I made it work. Katy Perry was the first official Facebook Live broadcast in January 2011. Millions of people tuned in. Her world tour sold out in minutes. From that point on, Facebook Live became a bona fide media outlet. Everyone wanted to take part. We had celebrities, politicians, athletes, world leaders—you name it—flocking to Facebook HQ to partake in Facebook Live.

Then, in April 2011, I got a call from the White House (who gets to say that other than Olivia Pope?!) because President Obama wanted to use Facebook Live to speak at a town hall with America. In fact, he loved the platform so much, the White House began doing a weekly Facebook Live video on important information and updates happening around the nation.

A few months later, I was nominated for an Emmy Award for Facebook Live, but lost to Anderson Cooper, reporting live from a ditch in Haiti. (You win this time, Cooper.) The most exciting event of all was when Facebook launched a Facebook Live button to *every single person* on Facebook (more than *two billion people*). This, from a tiny idea that I hacked together using my free time, soon became a pivotal part of Facebook. Even though I'm no longer with the company, every time I see an ad for Facebook Live in Times Square, or watch someone speaking directly to their followers and friends, I feel proud to have invented something so ubiquitously used by billions around the world. Without ever intending to, I left my own legacy on a company that has another, far more famous Zuckerberg at the helm.

So that's where it became pretty meta, I guess. My extracurricular work, which was supposed to be a fun break from my actual work, turned into so much work that I had to make a decision between focusing on my actual job, my side hustle job, or doing both and having no life. At a start-up, there's only one correct answer to this question: NO LIFE.

Well balanced wasn't even in my vocabulary during those years. When you're given the opportunity to work on something so massively successful, which also has such a tremendous impact on every industry and event, you don't think about balance. My work was my life. I worked around the clock for seven straight years. I traveled to over twenty countries *per year* for work. The weekend before I gave birth to my first son, I stayed up for three straight days, prepping for President Obama's Facebook Live broadcast at our office.

I loved being at Facebook. But I started to realize that when you work at a start-up you didn't start up yourself, you're lopsided toward somebody else's vision (even if it's family). Great leaders are excellent at getting thousands of people to see their vision so passionately that those people become lopsided in their leader's vision, too. But I couldn't shake my personal passions and dreams of what I wanted to be lopsided in. It wasn't someone else's vision that was driving me.

Now that I think back on it, this is the main reason the performing arts kept sneaking their way into *all* my work projects. First, the arts just hung out on the periphery, like Feedbomb, my eighties cover band. When I think about why I created Facebook Live, a big part was my own personal desire to produce and create a new channel for the arts.

I tried really, really, *really* hard to suppress the artistic part of me. In Silicon Valley you're supposed to be 100 percent focused on your start-up. If you aren't, you're looked at as a *faux-preneur*—a person who wants to lead but just doesn't have what it takes to do so. And personal passions and hobbies are considered the absolute worst distracting, frivolous, self-indulgent, not-what-it-takes qualities to have. Magnify those qualities tenfold if you're a woman, and a hundredfold if you have the last name Zuckerberg (hi!). There was (and still is) a serious case of Tall Poppy Syndrome in tech. The more ideas you have that create value and build your own personal brand, the more attention you draw to yourself. Draw attention to yourself, and eventually you're going to get chopped down to size.[5]

This was happening to me. The more I put myself out there, the more shade I got. Blog posts mocking "Mark Zuckerberg's sister who sings" flooded the interwebs. I had mentors give me advice to "be less interesting" if I wanted to succeed as a leader in the tech world, especially as a woman.

But I didn't want to be less interesting! Had I really worked this hard just to be invisible? To not reap any of the payoff of putting in all that time? To me, this is where so many companies get it wrong. They think that their employees work hard only for money, so if they just throw money at their workforce, those employees will continue to keep their heads down and be just as motivated. Until they aren't. Because we are human beings. We don't all work hard just for money. We work hard for all sorts of reasons: recognition, pride, acceptance, feeling like part of something bigger, a few seconds of fame or notoriety, strong work ethics, etc.

All of which are exactly why I left Silicon Valley for good when my number-one bucket list life dream presented itself to me: the chance to star on Broadway in *Rock of Ages*.

I spent my entire elementary school, middle school, high

school, and college years performing wherever and however I could. I was *sure* I was going to be a huge star! But life got in the way, and soon there I was, in my early thirties, working in tech, living in the California suburbs with my husband and our two-year-old son. I assumed my dream had long passed me by.

But that's the funny thing about dreams. Sometimes they come back and find you when you least expect it. One day, out of the blue, I got a phone call from Scott Prisand, one of the producers of *Rock of Ages*. They were looking for something "new and fresh" for the show and wanted to bring in a guest star—a tech personality. (*OMG. Was this the moment I'd been waiting for all my life?* Followed by . . . *Oh no! What if he asks for my brother's contact info!? I'll die!*) You can imagine my relief and exhilaration when Scott said several people had recommended ME. His offer was a leading role in a Broadway show!!

The only catch? I'd just found out that *same morning,* mere *hours* earlier, that I was pregnant with our second child.

It was a beautiful February California day (okay, every day in California is a beautiful day). Scott asked me if I'd be available in a few months, maybe May or June, to take the role. I quickly calculated when my belly would start showing. *Two plus six then carry the one . . .*

"How about this Monday?" I suggested.

After a short discussion with my husband, many tears of joy, and some consultation with my doctor, I was off to New York City a few days later—while my husband and toddler son stayed behind in California. Once I arrived in New York, I had a total of eight rehearsals before I made my Broadway debut in the role of Regina Koontz in *Rock of Ages*—exactly *three weeks* after receiving that phone call. It's hard to put into words what that experience was like, so I'll just say that it was one of the most incredible moments of my life. But not everyone agreed with my decision.

Several mentors advised me not to sing on Broadway, that I would never be taken seriously in business again if I left Silicon Valley to don a sparkly leotard and belt out "We're Not Gonna Take It." You know what I thought? I DON'T BUY IT. What was the point of continuously picking Work in my Pick Three if it only meant that I would have to keep picking it for the rest of my life at the expense of everything else? Hadn't I been so lopsided in Work so that when the time came to focus on something else, I had built up enough credibility, stockpiled enough Work Pick Threes? I was certain that at the end of my life I wouldn't be thinking, *Wow, I wish I hadn't sung on Broadway so I could try to please people who were never going to be pleased by me anyway.* That's how, after a decade of being incredibly lopsided toward other people's dreams and visions, I decided to focus on my own.

A study by the Association of Independent Professionals and the Self Employed (IPSE) found that 86 percent of nine hundred freelancers said they were "better off in terms of job satisfaction and similarly happier in life overall than being an employee doing something similar."[6] When I left Facebook, I started my own company, Zuckerberg Media, and immediately began consulting, speaking, and working for myself. Suddenly I could be lopsided however and whenever I wanted. It was liberating, exciting, and oh so freeing.

That said, I am NOT telling everyone who's unhappy at their job to quit. I know not everybody would have made the choice I made, but it was the right choice for ME. I wanted to start a family. I wanted to build my own company. Being lopsided can help you find your happiness, but everyone's version of being happy looks completely different, depending on where you are in your life. Your happiness may *or* may not be telling your boss to take your job and file it. (Though I do think more women should go start their own businesses!)

I know my story, but in no way do I claim to be an expert on Work, so I enlisted the help of a true **Work Expert,** MaryJo Fitzgerald—the corporate affairs and economic communications manager of one of the fastest growing job sites, Glassdoor—to weigh in. MaryJo told me there wasn't anything *wrong* with me for being a workaholic, but she encouraged me to redefine it as being "career oriented." However, that certainly doesn't mean focusing solely on your work and nothing else. "While there's nothing wrong with being career oriented," she said, "keeping balance in all aspects of your life is important!" She agreed with my theory of being well lopsided and not trying to have it all, at least not at the same time. "Allow yourself leeway when your focus needs to be on work, and when it needs to be on other aspects of your life."

In fact, she told me I was nowhere near alone in my career-oriented tendencies. According to a Glassdoor survey that MaryJo shared with me, Americans only take about half of their earned paid time off.[7] I was part of that statistic. One year, I had literally earned a free weeklong luxury cruise as part of a work project—and I never took it! I couldn't find one single week in the calendar year to take that damn vacation. Now, I'm kicking myself. What a fool! But in the moment, work seemed so important, with so many people depending on me, that I felt like I just couldn't step away.

MaryJo agrees with present-day Randi (and all of you) that yes, I was a fool. Okay, so maybe those weren't her words exactly, but she did say that taking a vacation is key to productivity. "Making time to put aside work and check out is important, and American workers aren't doing it enough . . . or at all," MaryJo says. "We are more productive when we have had time to step away—truly vacate—from our jobs." Maybe it's time to move to Fiji o'clock.

Working too hard without a break leads to all of us being far less effective in our jobs. MaryJo says the physical, mental, and emotional effects of overworking are terribly detrimental to the quality of our output. "If you're working ten, twelve, fourteen or more hours per day, you're no longer going to be effective at work. Our brains need time to rest so we can continue to be creative, strategic, and thoughtful. Find ways to be more efficient rather than simply burning the midnight oil. More hours spent working does not necessarily mean that you are a better worker. Quality over quantity."

Um, MaryJo, can you please tell that to my children? They're the most demanding bosses around!

The honest truth is that we all make our own choices. Which is wonderful. The amount that I pick Work in my Pick Three might feel way too lopsided for you. Stepping out of the workforce and not picking Work in Pick Three might feel like a saving grace for some but a horrible punishment for others. MaryJo says, "The idea of work-life balance is a very personal one, and reflecting on what your line is—when you may become unbalanced—is key. Know your limits and stick to them." I couldn't agree more. We all get to choose our own Pick Three.

Understanding yourself, your lifestyle, and the demands on

your time and attention can help you as you navigate the role of Work in your own Pick Three.

THE WORK PASSIONISTA

A person who chooses to be lopsided toward work makes a choice for themselves, not out of necessity or circumstance, and generally feels that they have the support of their friends, family, and/or community in making work a priority.

> *"One of my big frustrations about the way the media portrays single 'career' women is that we're all these crazy ambition monsters who chose not to get married and have a family. My least favorite meme is: 'She woke up at forty and realized she had forgotten to have a family!' Nobody hits forty and thinks, Oh my God, I forgot to have a baby."*
>
> **—MELINDA ARONS, FORMER DIRECTOR OF BROADCAST MEDIA FOR HILLARY FOR AMERICA**

After starring in *Rock of Ages* I was invited to be a correspondent for the Tony Awards, which meant interviewing stars and performers backstage—*five months pregnant*. I decided to go "in-tech-nito" to better distract attention from my belly, so I walked the red carpet wearing my Google Glass (the precursor to augmented reality glasses that had its fifteen minutes of fame—the Tony Awards happened at roughly minute 14:46 of that time frame). I was in my element. Theater plus tech plus Tonys, oh my!

In the Venn diagram of people who work in tech, people who are backstage at the Tony Awards, and Work Passionistas like myself, there are two people: myself and Melinda Arons. Melinda was overseeing creative video integration at my work alma mater, "The Book." That year she was responsible for getting Tony winners to post their thanks to fans on their Facebook pages. We bonded over being fellow theater/Facebook lovers, and from then on I was a Melinda Arons #fangirl.

Melinda Arons isn't a household name *yet* (just you wait!), which is precisely what drew me to speaking to her as a Work Passionista. Sure, we hear the stories of the same few dozen high-achieving famous names in business over and over again, but there are millions of us who love working hard, who are passionate about our careers, who make sacrifices in our lives in order to be career oriented. Most of us never get the same kind of notoriety, which, in a way, gives us more freedom to choose the Pick Three we want, because the world isn't watching our every move.

I could immediately relate to Melinda. She has always been drawn to high-pressure jobs, but she doesn't think she's super intense herself. She simply wants to be attached to things that are the best and hates to be associated with anything in which she hasn't given her all. Even in Melinda's personal life, she agonizes over which restaurant to go to, which vacation to take—she strives for perfection in everything she does.

Some might call this Type A; she calls it maximizing. Why waste the opportunity to have a good meal eating something average, especially if you can avoid it? She carries this philosophy into her professional career, thriving where the action is, surrounded by other high-performing people at the top of their game.

Melinda started her career at *Nightline,* where she played a pivotal role in revitalizing the show. From there, she went to work at Facebook, joining the company at the time of a high-growth sprint, post-IPO. All was going upward until a few years later, when Melinda left that high-profile job at Facebook in order to take a not-so-high-profile senior role on Hillary Clinton's 2016 presidential campaign.

Not many people would have had the guts to leave a big job like Melinda's. She described to me the lightning-speed time line in which she received the phone call from the Clinton campaign and was given five days to make the decision to pack her bags. In that time frame, you don't really have the luxury of weighing the pros and cons, you have to go with your gut. Melinda had always defined herself by her job titles, by the high-profile companies she worked for. She certainly was not the kind of person to make an irrational, spontaneous decision about anything—not which restaurant she was eating at and certainly not her career! Yet here she found herself making a risky, career-defining decision, with no time for data or lengthy conversations or weighing the pros and cons. A huge opportunity had presented itself, and in that situation a Work Passionista knows what has to be done.

(Melinda is the only person I know who'd leave an intense, demanding job at a tech company to work an even more intense, demanding job on a presidential campaign.)

Melinda took a huge gamble giving up the kind of job people work their whole lives to get, and all because she knew she couldn't watch such a monumental presidential campaign pass by without getting involved. She wouldn't have done it if it had been anyone else running for president. Melinda told me in our conversation that she would have gladly stuffed envelopes on that campaign and felt proud to do it. "The 2016 presidential election was a battle for the soul of the country," she told me. She felt that she couldn't wake up on Election Day and look herself in the mirror without knowing that she had given her all, worked for the outcome she wanted with the same focus and intensity as she had always approached her work.

But everything has a trade-off. Melinda acknowledges that she had to make some big sacrifices to be so focused on work. Which begs the question that every Work Passionista has to ask themselves at some point: *Is it worth it?*

(Especially considering her candidate didn't win.) (Written with a heavy sigh.)

For Work Passionistas, often our biggest strength and biggest weakness are the same thing. Our intense drive and motivation to succeed propels us to incredible heights in our careers, yet can also blind us to some of the other aspects of our lives that we might be ignoring.

The question *Is it worth it?* is one that we all ask ourselves, at many different points in our lives. And it's certainly a question that anyone who makes a drastic career jump must ask themselves (as both Melinda and I had done, jumping from Facebook to politics and Broadway, respectively). For Melinda, the answer is a resounding yes. It was worth it in spades. Even though the election didn't have the outcome she had hoped for, she was proud of herself for taking a huge risk and diving into the unknown headfirst. "I finally felt like I had broken free from having my self-worth associated with big-name companies."

But anytime you're *that* lopsided in one thing, you have to look at the full picture, and for Melinda, an intense focus on her career coupled with the fact that she was living in big cities where "men really do not have to 'settle down' in a timely manner, if ever," turned into an all-too-familiar-for-many vicious cycle. "You're working crazy hard, and you haven't met the right person yet. But then, because you haven't met the right person yet, you work even harder to fill the void." Melinda told me stories of how she truly felt for the struggles of working moms but, at the same time, why did nobody ever ask her about balance? Why was work-life balance only a question for people with children? Why was she always the one expected to work late hours because she didn't have a soccer game to run home to? Didn't people appreciate that she also wanted to go out and have a life, so that one day she could also feel that same mommy guilt to rush home to a soccer game?

Melinda felt constant anxiety over the fact that her Pick Three was being decided for her—not by her—by people who had chosen their own priorities. Which compounded her mixed feelings of wanting to pick Family, just not sure if it was in the cards for her. "I want to have children," she said. "I just really don't want to do it alone."

Now Melinda is taking a break in her career, for the first time ever. After the extreme intensity of the campaign and the disappointing conclusion, she felt she needed some time to reflect. Not for long, I'm sure. Work Passionistas never do last long out of their native habitat of the workforce. In fact, by the time you're reading this, she's likely leapt right back into a high-pressure, intense work environment. But the year off has already done wonders for her. When I spoke to her, she looked refreshed, energized, and relaxed. She told me that for the first time in her life, Work wasn't in her Pick Three. She was focusing on Friends, Sleep, and Family. "I know that sounds strange to hear from a woman my age without children, but one of the things I am most proud of is my relationship with my family."

She also acknowledged that her age had something to do with her ability to take that break. She felt like all the hard work she had logged in her twenties and thirties, the years of intense commitment and long hours, had given her the credibility and the reputation to be able to take some time off without judgment. It also boosted confidence in her ability to jump right back into being a Work Passionista when she was good and ready. She told me that if she were in her twenties she wouldn't have felt like she could take this time off and, quite frankly, she said, "I wouldn't have deserved it."

If you can relate to being the Work Passionista, that's fantastic! It's wonderful to value your career and make it a focal point of your life and identity. On the positive side, you're likely destined for career greatness! Just remember that any time you're consistently and repeatedly lopsided in one area of your life, it means that you only have *Pick Two* left, so it's important to make sure you're shuffling through Work, Sleep, Family, Fitness, and Friends, in as equal a way as possible. For Work Passionistas, it's really easy to burn out if you bite off more than you can chew—especially if Work is the meat, potatoes, salad, and dessert of your meal. If you can, try to take at least one day each week where you don't choose Work at all.

On the complete other side of the spectrum, there's the viewpoint of people who live an incredibly rich and meaningful life without ever prioritizing Work—people who focus and Pick Three by choosing what *not* to do, becoming lopsided by process of elimination, removing Work as a category they ever have to choose.

TAKE YOUR WORK GAME TO THE NEXT LEVEL (WITHOUT BURNING OUT)

If you're a Work Passionista and you want to take your job to the next level in a way that doesn't necessarily mean putting more hours in at the office, here are a few great tips:

BE A THOUGHT LEADER. If you want to be known as an expert in your field, you have to create content that helps other people. Luckily, there are so many easy ways to set up your own blog, or author posts on popular social media sites. Weighing in on current events in your industry, writing thought pieces, or sharing your own tips can be a great way to go from superstar employee to bona fide expert in your field, without taking up tons of extra time. (I know you're busy, Passionistas!) I recommend posting something at least once or twice a month.

LEARN HOW TO BE A GREAT PRESENTER. You can be the greatest employee in the world, but if you don't know how to present your ideas in an effective, compelling way, you'll find that you eventually hit a ceiling in your career. I've seen way too many excellent entrepreneurs whose presentation skills hinder their ability to raise funding and recruit awesome candidates. Working with a presentation coach, joining a public speaking group, or even taking an improv class can make the difference between getting your startup funded, pitching and getting a new client, getting your idea green lit, or landing that next big raise or promotion.

GET COMFORTABLE DELEGATING. One thing about Work Passionistas: we love to do it all. But you're never going to level up in your career if you don't start offloading smaller tasks that allow you to focus on the bigger strategic ones. There are several tools in the marketplace that allow you to hire a virtual assistant to help you with basic tasks, freeing you up to take on more challenging assignments. Perform a cost/benefit analysis for tasks like housekeeping and cooking. Would the hours you saved from those tasks be worth outsourcing?

JUST SAY "NO." This one seems a bit counterintuitive (won't people be impressed if you take on more work?), but learning what to say "no" to is even more important than saying "yes." Of course certain people are more difficult to say "no" to (i.e., your boss), but the higher you climb in your career, the more distracting things will get dangled in front of you. Lots of people want you to spend time helping them with their goals. Keep your eyes on the prize and stay ruthlessly focused on your goals. The better you do for you, the more you'll be able to help others.

BECOME AN E-MAIL NINJA. I know you probably have a ton of e-mails to get through. Not to mention texts, posts, and all the other messages cluttering your gadgets. Train yourself to keep your e-mail communication as short as possible. If you have the type of schedule that allows it, train yourself to answer e-mail in batches, opening your e-mail only a few times a day, instead of a constant stream of disruption all day long. It goes without saying that anything remotely emotional or sensitive should always be done via phone, video chat, or in person.

THE WORK ELIMINATOR

A person who makes a conscious choice NOT to focus on Work, by retiring, taking time off, staying home as a caregiver, etc. This person may or may not know what they want to be lopsided in. Regardless, they know that Work isn't it and that they don't want to be defined by a job or career.

> *"It was less judgmental than it was today. Many more women stayed at home. The ones I became good friends with, we had all given up successful careers. We were all-in on our family. I felt for the moms who tried to do both. Someone would have a court case and a child was throwing up and it just tore them to pieces."*
>
> **—KAREN ZUCKERBERG,**
> **PSYCHIATRIST AND MOTHER OF FOUR**

There are many reasons people become Work Eliminators. Some people feel like they have a calling in an area outside of Work. Some people find themselves in a financial or life situation where they have to stay at home as a caregiver. Some people have worked hard for many years and are now enjoying the fruits of retirement. Some people have a spouse who is a Work Passionista, which affords them the opportunity to direct their energy toward home.

Whatever the reason, most people don't want to pick Work every single day of their lives. And that's a good thing. But there's a difference between simply taking a short career break and being a long-term Work Eliminator, and I really wanted to understand what drives people to become the latter.

There's no one better I could have learned from about making the conscious decision to eliminate Work as one of their Pick

Three, either for a period of time or for good, than the most bad-ass, intelligent stay-at-home parent I know—my mom, Karen Zuckerberg.

My mother was on track to be an accomplished physician. She was valedictorian of her school, and, in true supermom form, despite having two children while in medical school and dealing with sexist comments left and right in a male-dominated field, she still graduated with flying colors. After graduation she went through several more years of residency, pulling multiple weekly all-nighters at the hospital—only to step away from all of it to become a full-time parent. After investing years of time and energy in her education and training, she realized that she didn't want to pick Work, she wanted to stay at home and focus on her children. She knew that there would be people in her life who wouldn't like that decision, or who would put pressure on her to finish what she had started, but she also knew that it was her life and she wanted to live without regretting her choices. Working late at the hospital when she had young children at home had left her with too many regrets.

I asked my mom why. Why would she do that? Why invest all that time, money, and sweat just to quit ten yards from the finish line? Did she ever wish she had stuck with her career? It was interesting to be sitting down with my mom discussing this because basically I was asking her, "Was it worth it to give up your career—for me?" I had never had such a candid conversation with my mother about her own goals and aspirations. And those include the trade-offs she had made to be such an involved parental figure.

She said that before having kids, she wouldn't have been able to understand her line of thinking, either. She had no idea what it was going to be like being a parent until she was one. What she thought would be an easy decision—*of course she would return to work*—became quite painful and difficult. She found that she hated leaving her children with someone she didn't really know. So when push came to shove, she stepped away from her career in order to stay at home.

There are real detrimental effects of mommy guilt. Guilt keeps us from truly focusing and feeling good about our successes and can cripple our forward momentum in our Pick Three progress. Maybe I'm not one to talk; I beat myself up with mommy guilt every time I take a business trip and miss our bedtime routine. This past Mother's Day I wore a T-shirt that said WORLD'S OKAYEST MOM, which is all too true. But the real truth is that being a good parent doesn't necessarily mean choosing your family as your number-one priority every day of your life, it just means making sure you're completely present and engaged when you are around.

All in all, it seems like my mother is quite happy with her decision. After all, I think we all turned out okay. But it was a bit difficult to hear her talk about feeling judged at cocktail parties, how people would talk to her for two seconds, hear that she was "just a mom," and quickly walk away to go talk to someone else more "useful." It seemed like she had many years in which her entire self-worth was completely wrapped up in her children and their accomplishments. When I asked if she had any regrets, she teared up a bit, talking about the life she always thought she would have, with her own private psychiatry practice, and told me, "Of course I do. But if I had to do it all over again, I wouldn't change a thing." Aw, thanks, Mom.

However, when I asked her what she would tell one of her

own daughters if they told her they wanted to follow in her foot-steps and be a stay-at-home mom like her, she told me she'd have to think about it. After a long pause, she said, "I'd be support-ive of their decision, but I would strongly encourage them to have something of their own going on. Something they could fall back on if needed. A passion or interest that gives them an identity separate from just having children."

She was also quick to recognize that many people do find that deeper passion and meaning in their family and that step-ping away from work is absolutely the right decision for them. "The key is to find what you are passionate about. By having a passion in your life, you have a goal to work hard toward. It gives you meaning." So if, like my own mother, your passion is for be-ing there for your family, that's a beautiful thing.

I was shocked (and a little guilty) to also hear my mom say that the hardest thing about being a stay-at-home mom is hav-ing your children grow up, move across the country with your grandkids, and never call or text. (Umm, who could she possibly be talking about?) Choking up a bit, she explained, "Motherhood is a job that, if you do really well, you're no longer as needed." I'd beg to differ. No matter where you go in life, no matter what you do, mom is always needed.

"Just looking at the adults my children have become, I'm so proud of every single one of them. I can't believe how incredibly blessed I am," my mom shared at the end of our interview. All I can say is that I am definitely the one who is blessed. I can only hope that my own sons feel the same way about me one day. Even though I am not a Work Eliminator, by the end of our dis-cussion, I had a real understanding and connection for why so many people would make that choice. (Also, at the conclusion of our chat, I pulled out my phone to prove to her that I did in fact contact her *at least* every two days!)

But what if you were once a Work Eliminator and have now changed your mind and want to reenter the workforce? Of course, there are many situations where that makes sense. Children grow up. Financial and marital situations change. A chance to dust off that ol' master's degree is suddenly a welcome adventure.

According to a study published by the *Harvard Business Review,* 37 percent of qualified women leave their jobs for extended periods of time. Of those women, only 40 percent find full-time jobs again, 23 percent find part-time work, 7 percent are self-employed, and 30 percent don't return to the workforce at all.[8] More than three million women with college or advanced degrees are currently trying to find jobs, says Jennifer Gefsky, co-founder and CEO of Après, the staffing and recruiting company for women reentering the workforce.

I recently had Jennifer as a guest on my SiriusXM business radio show, where she gave advice to parents who had previously been Work Eliminators and now wanted to pick Work in their Pick Three once again. "Career gaps should be embraced," she told my listeners. "Don't run away from the résumé gap. We know it! It's okay! Just own it."

If anyone knows, it's Jennifer. She left a huge job as the former deputy general counsel (and highest-ranking woman) in Major League Baseball, in order to stay at home. Reentering the workforce with gusto, Jennifer started her own company. She claims that businesses don't put enough value on the school of life. "Life experience is huge! I have so much more to offer now than I did at thirty-five!"

Jennifer had some excellent tips for those who think they

might take some time as a Work Eliminator. For instance, if you're going to step out of the workforce and think there's *even a fraction of a chance* you might want to go back and become lopsided toward Work again, it's important to think about how you can still maintain your skills and keep a foot in the door. But Jennifer warns that certain skills and associations are more valuable than others. I was shocked to hear her say, "If you have PTA on your résumé, there's a huge chance that résumé will go straight in the trash can. But if you put 'I raised $100,000 for our local school,' then that's a transferable skill that is considered valuable in any business setting."

When I had my second son, I decided to take some time off from work—three whole months, which felt downright luxurious, considering I had never taken so much as even a *three-week* vacation up until then. I know it should be standard, believe me, but that's a whole different topic for a different book.

Voluntarily removing myself from my job for an extended time felt a bit foreign to a workaholic like me. Also, let's remember I was working for myself by then as well, so taking time off means no clients, which means no income—exactly what Jennifer Gefsky of Après had gone through when she left MLB.

Jennifer says that when we make the decision to leave the workforce, we need to make the decision with our eyes wide open. Your current salary might not be enough to cover a full-time nanny, and therefore, you're better off at home. But then we forget that salaries increase over time, plus all the other benefits like health care, 401(k)s, etc. You might not feel a difference with your salary today, right this second. But Jennifer urges, "The exponential loss of incoming money will make an impact"—and it might take years to realize it. So before you make the decision to be a Work Eliminator, it's important to understand exactly what you're up against.

Prior to my self-enforced maternity leave I'd been in discussions with SiriusXM about starting my own business talk show. They offered to set up recording equipment in my house so I could start during my leave. After some thought, I realized that this was the perfect way to keep my foot in the door while I was taking time to focus on the new baby.

Just one hour a week on the radio would allow me to stay up-to-date on the latest business news and trends, and maintain relevancy in my network. Thinking about little things you can do to keep the conversation going and maintain contacts will go a long way in the future, especially if you ever want to access those networks again. It might not be feasible for every single person to start their own radio show. (Although why not! There are more than a million podcasts in the iTunes store!) Jennifer suggests making it a priority to have at least one networking meeting or phone call on your calendar each week. And to think about keeping your toe in the water by starting a blog, becoming active with a nonprofit, or maintaining a regular professional LinkedIn account.

And let me speak to all the incredible men out there who are Work Eliminators and caregivers: advice relating to career gaps and how to reenter the workforce applies to everyone, not just women. A Pew Research Center report estimates that two million U.S. fathers with children aren't working outside the home.[9] Of these, 21 percent, or an estimated 420,000 men, say they are home to care for family. This percentage is a fourfold increase from 1989, when only 5 percent of men claimed full-time care-giving as their reason for not working outside the home. Men are definitely not absent from the stay-at-home-parent equation, and we salute your efforts!

If you can relate to being a Work Eliminator, either a temporary one like Jennifer or a permanent one like my mother, I take my hat off to you. The people in your life are very lucky to have you. The wonderful thing about eliminating work is that your relationships often pay off abundantly (my mother is one of my very best friends), resulting in lasting value that's priceless.

I want to caution Eliminators—especially after speaking with both my mother and Jennifer—to make sure that your identity and self-worth do not get *too* tied up in other people. We can't control what other people do or how appreciative they are, no matter how much love, time, and energy we put into those people. Both Jennifer and my mom echo the sentiment that for Work Eliminators, it's crucial to have your own personal projects or hobbies and to try to dip at least one pinky toe in the water with professional contacts if you think there's even the slightest possibility you might want to be lopsided toward Work in the future. As Jennifer puts it, "Know the price you're paying for what you're doing. Keep a foot in the door. Do something once a week to keep going."

My mom, the quintessential New Yorker, put it a bit more bluntly. "If you don't have something of your own going on, you won't be interesting to people, and they won't want to connect with you." And, if and when you DO decide to go back to the workforce, don't delay—just get started. Good things happen when you put yourself out there.

KEEPING THE DOOR OPEN

Many people take a break from their careers. Sometimes it's a short break, sometimes an extended one. If you think there's even the slightest chance you might want to return to work one day, here are a few ways to keep one foot in the door so that it's much easier to reprioritize your career if you choose to do so.

READ. A LOT. Stay informed on current events and industry trends so you can have an intelligent conversation with people who could become valuable connections. If things you're reading and learning about make you feel so inclined, play around with the idea of writing the occasional blog post or starting your own podcast on a topic of your interest and expertise.

MAINTAIN YOUR CONNECTIONS. Make sure you don't lose touch with former employers and colleagues who might need to serve as a reference or make introductions for you one day. Make sure you at least lightly stay in touch with your professional network on social media, send holiday cards, and pick up the phone at least once or twice a year to say "hi."

TAKE ON A VOLUNTEER POSITION. But do it strategically. Depending on what industry in which you want to stay connected, certain volunteer activities will be viewed as more transferable and applicable than others.

KEEP UP WITH TECH. Has the technology in your industry been changing? Make sure you stay up to date on changes, even if it means taking an occasional class or getting a tutor. The better you keep up, the less overwhelming it will be to try to reenter a career where all the tools of the trade have completely changed.

BECOME AN INTERN AGAIN. Don't be afraid of unpaid, temporary, or part-time positions. Maybe you have children going away to camp for the summer? Maybe you have some extra time in the mornings? Maybe you're able to work a few hours from home? Some companies have more formal "returnships"-intern programs for people coming back from a career break.

THE WORK RENOVATOR

Someone who hits a roadblock that causes him/her to have to rebuild and refocus career plans.

> *"Failure can be a blessing. I don't even realize the times when I do things that are seemingly brave. Losing the election was such a gift. I didn't die, and I live a life that's honest enough. It doesn't mean there aren't consequences, but I don't feel duplicitous."*
>
> **—RESHMA SAUJANI, FOUNDER OF GIRLS WHO CODE**

It can be difficult to reinvent yourself in your career. Sometimes no matter what you do, no matter how hard you try, you just keep hitting wall after wall after wall. After I left Facebook, I had moments of crippling insecurity when I worried no one would care about me if I was no longer tied to one of the hottest global companies in the world. Would I ever be anything except for somebody's sister?

A few weeks ago, I was on CNBC discussing an exciting new

project I was launching, something that has absolutely nothing to do with Facebook whatsoever. Yet the anchor introduced me by saying, "Mark Zuckerberg's sister is here in the studio with us today." So I replied, "Sorry, I haven't legally changed my name to 'Mark Zuckerberg's sister' yet, so please just call me Randi." It's taken me a few years of moving to a different coast and having several successes all on my own, but now I truly have the confidence to embrace my personal reinvention.

Most of us are somewhere in the process of reinventing ourselves. Perhaps that's why you're reading this book—to learn how to better restructure your career, rebrand your life, shift gears. The world is changing so quickly that people who dedicated their entire careers to one company now suddenly find themselves out of a job when their company goes under. People who chose what would normally be evergreen, "safe" jobs are now seeing that no position is truly safe in the tech era. The world is full of motivated, ambitious people who have been forced to become Work Renovators.

Take Reshma Saujani, the founder of Girls Who Code. I first met Reshma in 2010, when she was running for Congress. In fact, the first political campaign I ever donated to was Reshma's! Even though she didn't win that election—or her following run for New York City public advocate—Reshma's passion for community leadership and change shone through, and I was proud to support a young woman running on such an ambitious platform.

It would have been easy to get jaded after losing two elections in such a short period of time. I mean, a regular person can hit a brick wall and face public rejection only so many times before they give up, but, luckily, Reshma is not a regular person.

She stuck with her decision to give back via public service and was able to reinvent herself in one of the most masterful pivots I have seen: as the founder of Girls Who Code, a nonprofit that teaches programming to young women in order to increase the number of women working in computer science. A true Work Renovator in every sense.

Reshma pivoted her career after her two-time defeat. She jokes that it wasn't really even a choice. When I spoke with her she said that each time she lost a campaign, Girls Who Code got bigger, growing with every setback. Although her mission was always to launch GWC, her initial plan was for someone else to run the organization while she spent her own career working in public service. "But I guess that was never God's plan, or anyone else's plan," Reshma admitted. "When I lost my public advocate race and got shut down on getting computer science into every classroom, I said, 'F you. I'm going to do this on my own and build this massive movement.'" Where many would have backed down, Reshma instead reached even higher, using the pain from her failures to create something larger than anyone had expected.

Years later, Reshma says she can finally admit that losing the election was like a gift. While, of course, she was disappointed and had to reconcile that she might never have the life in politics she had always dreamed of, she still felt that at the end of the day she could hold her head high because *she'd tried.* She went for it. The vast majority of people would have been too scared to even step into the ring.

I speak to many successful people every week on my SiriusXM show, and most of these entrepreneurs have faced failure, rejection, and disappointment. It's how you respond to that failure, how your inner Work Renovator starts rearranging the pieces, that truly defines you in that moment. Reshma's experiences helped her redefine what success means to her, and that success now means running an incredible organization that creates opportunities for girls that wasn't available before.

Recently Reshma became a mother, which added a whole list of joys—and challenges. Reshma and I joked about the mommy guilt we feel when we leave on business trips. She quoted Arianna Huffington, who said, "We take the baby out, and we put the guilt in." Reshma told me a story about a time she decided to bring her son along to an event she was speaking at. Her nanny had a last-minute emergency and couldn't watch Reshma's son on the day of the event. "I'm about to go onstage and address all the governors of the country and my son starts having a fit," she told me, describing a situation that would make pretty much any parent cringe with understanding. Kids always have such impeccable timing! "My team's looking at me like, 'Whoa.' And of course in my mind I'm like, 'Why do I do this to myself? I could've left him at home.' I'm happier when I'm with him, but that often creates more chaos."

All kidding aside, I truly appreciated Reshma's parting wisdom to me about how she constantly asks herself how she can be better and how she constantly pushes herself outside her comfort zone to the edge of her ability. She's found that as she's gotten older, she rarely does things that make her comfortable, and that those moments where she's testing her limits are truly what make her feel alive.

WHEN TO BREAK UP WITH A CLIENT

Sometimes if you work for yourself or are a freelancer, being a Work Renovator means knowing when you have to move on from a difficult client. It may seem like a first-world problem to have to turn down business, but time and talent are things you should never be okay with someone else taking from you.

I was flown out to New Delhi for a tech conference a few years ago. I flew halfway around the world to give a thirty-minute keynote about the future of social media and its importance to Digital India—an initiative to advance the tech infrastructure to all Indian citizens by 2019. The conference sounded exciting and definitely within my wheelhouse. I was proud to be asked to be part of a panel that included the head of Google India, who was making sweeping digital advances in the country.

But once I got to India, it was a different story entirely. India is still a male-dominated country, and I heard from a few Indian women that they had "many, many, MANY glass ceilings to break there." My speech was cut down from thirty minutes to *six* minutes because the man speaking before me went over his time. During our Digital India panel, I was the sole woman present and I was only asked ONE question: how I balanced having children and working (go figure), a question that made my eyes roll and that none of the male panelists were asked. So yes, I got paid for that trip, but did I feel good about earning that money? NO. I felt underutilized and embarrassed.

MORAL OF THE STORY: if you work for yourself, value yourself. Establish your rates. Find that number you can say without laughing . . . then add a little bit more. (I'm looking at you, ladies!) The more you set some ground rules and stick to them, the more others will value your time as well. And if a client isn't working out, well, sometimes renovating means doing some spring cleaning.

Can't we all relate to the Work Renovator? We have dreams of what we want to be when we grow up, what we're going to do—then life happens. When you read about great entrepreneurs, you'll often hear about the concept of "pivoting," or being able to react quickly and swiftly to changes in the market in order to set your business on the right track, even if it means scrapping your original plans and doing something completely different. Well, human beings pivot, too. Very few of us are doing today what we thought we'd be doing when we were children. (I thought I was going to be a mermaid!) All of us hit roadblocks and obstacles.

Work Renovators like Reshma are resilient, they are bold, they know how to pick up the pieces of their professional life that work—and how to walk away from what isn't working. Lots of people get stuck. It's difficult to venture out into the uncomfortable, the unknown, but Renovators are resourceful. Had Reshma not experienced those defeats, she wouldn't have been able to conquer them, achieving the success that brought about great change both for her career and for the world.

THE ART OF THE PIVOT

There's no perfect time to make a career pivot. Sometimes it's by choice, sometimes a wrench unexpectedly gets thrown into our employment plans. But if you wake up and realize your career is on the wrong track, then by all means do something about it! You're not alone. Most of us, at one point or another, will make a career switch, change jobs within the same company, decide to freelance, or even start our own venture.

GET ADVICE FROM OTHERS, BUT *YOUR* THOUGHTS MATTER MOST.
Lots of people will tell you the many things that could go wrong. It's usually a mix of them being risk-averse because they love you (and change is scary) stirred in with some jealousy because they probably wish they could make a big change, too. If your heart tells you it's time for a career pivot, don't let other people's fears dissuade you.

TAKE STOCK OF YOUR SKILL SET AND WHAT YOU LOVE DOING.
Chances are good that once you pinpoint what you enjoy doing and what you're good at, you'll be able to find several industries that utilize those skills. Network with others in those industries or attend local meetups to figure out what skills you might need to catch up on.

UPDATE YOUR PROFILES. Make sure any website or social media account others can find via Google is updated often and refers to your projects and skill sets. Just because you've mentally begun the process of pivoting doesn't mean that everyone else knows!

TIMING IS KEY. If you're going to start talking about making changes publicly, make sure you're ready to follow through. If people send you leads for new jobs, clients, or opportunities and you don't follow up, you'll find that people become less likely to want to help a second time around. Have a clear plan of action so you can act on leads that come in.

JUST DO IT. Honestly, sometimes the best thing to do for your life, for your soul, is to make big changes and go for it. Don't drag it out. If you know you want to do something, then your heart and mind are already made up, you just need to take the leap. The worst thing that can happen is that it doesn't work out and you find another job. There's never been a better time to take risks. I'm excited for you!

THE WORK SUPERHERO

A person who becomes lopsided toward Work in support of someone they love—a spouse, a dear friend, a family business, etc. No capes necessary.

> *"As the years have ticked by there's something in our chemistry that is abnormal in the sense that we're together 24/7. So many couples split up during the day. We never escape from each other. I don't know if that's good or bad. But it works for us."*
>
> **—BRAD TAKEI, BUSINESS MANAGER AND HUSBAND OF GEORGE TAKEI**

Sometimes we become lopsided not for ourselves, but for the people we love. My husband is someone who truly embodies this. When I received that phone call to sing on Broadway, suddenly my husband turned into a single parent in California—and he supported my decision every step of the way.

For my final performance he flew to New York to see the show again (his *sixth* time, I believe). After the show he helped pack my things up for my return home. Even though I was ecstatic to return to my family, I cried the entire taxi ride to the airport. Like, ugly cried. The cabdriver had to turn up the volume on the radio, I was sobbing so hard. To this day I can't hear John Legend's "All of Me" without weeping.

By the time the plane touched down, my husband proposed that we consider moving back to New York City, permanently. Even though he didn't know if he would have the same career options as in Silicon Valley, he told me I seemed lighter in my soul. "You love theater," he said. "How can someone like you be happy living in suburban California? I'll find a great company to work for. We'll find a great school for the boys. Let's do this." So we did.

(For context on how über lucky I am, this is the same man who turned down his dream job in California to stay with me when I lived in New York after college. A few months after the job offer had passed, I decided to move to California to work with my brother at "The Facebook." After a year of long distance, my husband moved out to California to join me. You can see why I married the guy!)

In the summer of 2015, we moved to New York City and never looked back. (Well, okay, maybe a few times in bitter-cold February, we *may* have questioned our decision.) Now I'm a voter for the Tony Awards and the Chita Rivera Awards. I'm happily required to see sixty shows a year. My husband—who couldn't even name three musicals when we first started dating and could count the total number of theatrical shows he had seen on one finger, now spends most of his weekends seeing shows with me. He can name every Broadway show that's come out in the past five years and has a knowledge of show tunes that could rival Kristin Chenoweth's.

These same traits of my husband embody the Work Superhero—someone who is lopsided toward Work to support the career passions of the person they love deeply. Aside from my husband, there is nobody who embodies this role with more grace, passion, and enthusiasm than Brad Takei.

Most people know Brad's famous husband, George Takei, and his groundbreaking role as Mr. Hikaru Sulu, the helmsman of the USS *Enterprise* in *Star Trek*. Brad and George have been married for nine years and together for thirty. Brad has endured the ups and downs of a Hollywood career, providing encouragement and guidance and, in many ways, changing his own identity to support his husband's.

George and Brad met in the early eighties, when Brad was a full-time print journalist. When he met George, Brad was a recreational runner, something George was also passionate about. They met through LA Frontrunners, a gay and lesbian social running club. They ran around the Silver Lake reservoir and the rest was history. They kept their relationship a secret for eighteen years. In 2008, George and Brad legally married after being domestic partners for two decades.

Brad didn't always work as George's business manager. He valued his career as a journalist and loved his work. But little by little, their relationship started to shift from being life partners to becoming coworkers as well. Brad started to realize how detail oriented he was in comparison with George, who got lost in lofty artistic and intellectual concepts. "He's always got these big ideas, but is he going to make that flight on time? As a journalist I'm detail oriented and do great bookkeeping. We became a good combination. So, from the nineties onward, we've been Team Takei. Taking the ups and downs of life and work."

George is seventeen years older than Brad and has acted as a mentor, while George sees Brad as his reliable Rock of Gibraltar. "Every morning I always bring George a cup of hot green tea and the print edition of the *New York Times* when it's available. We end our day, even if we've had any spats or conflicts, with a kiss before we go to sleep."

George is the brand of Team Takei, so when Brad and George attend sci-fi conventions, George, one of four original *Star Trek* cast members still alive, is often the center of attention. "A couple of decades ago I was in the shadows, but George has made a point to share his life with people. Since we're always together, he's inclusive about me. Now people want my picture, too. I have just enough introvert in my personality to be fine with George being the center of attention. I've always been blessed, I've never felt jealous."

Brad and George have a wonderful working relationship because they have a strong personal relationship. Brad feels that being together 24/7 is actually a relationship saver, because they can address everything in real time so they're always on top of things. "The truth is, we had to make choices all along to get to where we are. The dirty secret of our personal and business life, the reason it works so well, is that we are both workaholics." (I corrected him: they're both Work Passionistas!)

George was already a household name when he and Brad met. In 1965, the creator of *Star Trek,* Gene Roddenberry, cast George as Hikaru Sulu, which suddenly provided George with a megaphone where millions of people were listening. He wanted to use that megaphone for something meaningful, so he began telling the story of the Japanese American internment camps he grew up in as a child in America. When Brad and George met later on, Brad understood that supporting George meant supporting George's passions, so as part of #TeamTakei, Brad championed his husband's decision to use his celebrity to speak out against inequality and the lesser-known horrors of American history. "If you don't use the platform you're given, you're not helping. When forced into the position of doing the right thing, it can be both challenging and rewarding at times."

Brad is happy being George's middleman between Hollywood and the outside world. He provides George with everything from Kleenex to vitamins to green tea. "I think to myself, we've never had a marriage counselor or therapy in our life because I can forget about the petty stuff. George is an artist, so I let him have his space. Maturity is really helpful. I made my life commitment to George in my thirties. When it was time for George to settle down in his forties, it was a commitment. I don't really understand divorce too much. I'm a child of divorce. And I couldn't imagine separating from George. I made a commitment to this person. It's not about me. It's about us."

The saddest part for George and Brad was that when they got together, LGBT people in America faced more obstacles than they do now. George was in his late forties, Brad in his early thirties, and they knew they would never have children together. "We were closeted gay men at the time, so it would have been unfair to the kids. . . . If you know George and me, what great parents we would've been. We have younger kids in our life we get to shower our affections on. George loves kids and would've been a great father. We don't have the energy now, at eighty and sixty-three."

If you can relate to Brad or my husband, and feel like you have changed your course or shifted your career to accommodate someone in your own life, then clearly you're a Superhero! It's a wonderful thing to be able to give so freely of yourself and apply your business skills in a way that benefits someone you love so dearly. In fact, you're making me feel like I should probably go give my husband a big hug right about now, because it is impossible to accomplish anything in life without a strong support system—if you're a Work Superhero, then that's you!

This entire book is about Pick Three, and you've pretty much beaten me at my own game because you've already accomplished a major life hack by picking two things at once, so congrats!

That said, it's important, too, that your independent sense of identity stays strong and you keep at least one or two interests that are solely for yourself—whether that's a fitness routine, a genre of music, or a book you're reading. It's very easy to allow your identity to get swallowed up by someone you love and support, especially when your career decisions all come back to that person you love. (Not that I know *anything* about being involved in a family business and starting to lose your own identity—Oh wait, I do.)

Brad Takei admitted his secret way of getting in some of his own Brad time: reality television! "I download reality TV shows on my iPhone—*Housewives, Survivor*—at night while [George] is reading Japanese novels that help him intellectually. He has no interest in reality TV. . . . He also loves going to see Shakespeare. For me it's like watching paint dry."

It took me a few *years* post-Facebook to feel like I was back on the path to having my own identity. Hopefully you make sure to keep a few interests and activities that are just for you, even if you find incredible meaning in helping someone else achieve their career dreams.

THE ART OF THE SIDE HUSTLE

Actor/singer or writer/director—it used to be that only entertainers could add the *slash* in their career summary. But nowadays it's becoming more common that people pay the bills with their nine-to-five job and fulfill their dreams from five to nine. It's called side hustling, and it can actually become so lucrative that you can quit your day job to follow your passion.

Take *Shark Tank*'s Daymond John, who worked at Red Lobster for four years while trying to build his clothing brand FUBU, which is now worth millions. Or actor/physician Ken Jeong, of the *Hangover* franchise. Jeong was a licensed doctor, performing stand-up on the side, when he got cast in Judd Apatow's *Knocked Up,* and his career soared up from there. Side hustling is not as simple as ignoring your day job and pinning all your hopes on one prospect. Just ask Hulk Hogan, whose Pastamania restaurant lasted less than a year in business.

Tina Yip is the cocreator of *5to9,* a podcast for those looking to pave the way for their dreams while working a regular nine-to-five.

 "Having a side hustle is a great way to explore your passions. It's a blank canvas that is 100 percent you. No one is judging you, and you can do whatever you want with it! No matter how much you love your job, you're making someone else's dream happen. With your side project, you're making your dreams happen at minimal cost. It's where you can be 100 percent you. . . . The tough reality is that because of survival and economic needs, we're forced to follow career paths and opportunities that value making money more than doing what we love. To make our careers closer to our passions, we need to be creative and find ways to integrate the two."

FOUR WAYS TO CREATE YOUR OWN SIDE HUSTLE:

1. **IDENTIFY THE PURPOSE AND ASK YOURSELF WHY:** Whenever you have an idea about a project, ask yourself why you want to do it and how it serves a greater purpose in helping you be who you want to be. A lot of side projects lose steam because people simply go with their first instinct and realize soon after that they don't really want to work on it. But by all means, if the purpose of your side hustle time is to experiment with as many things as possible that struck a chord with you, then go for it!

2. **STAY ACCOUNTABLE WITH A THIRTY-DAY OR ONE-HUNDRED-DAY PROJECT:** This is a great way to structure your side hustles and keep yourself accountable.

3. **COMMIT BY SETTING SIDE HUSTLE MEETINGS AND BUDGETS:** Treat your side hustle time like a real appointment. If you can make an appointment for your mani/pedi and show up, you can set aside side hustle time.

4. **TELL AS MANY PEOPLE AS POSSIBLE:** Because you never know how much people are willing to help.

THE WORK MONETIZER

Someone who creates a business around the fact that other people want to pick Work in their Pick Three. They help other people become lopsided toward Work—and make money in the process!

"My only regret is that I didn't become an entrepreneur sooner in life. I could have left the corporate world years earlier. I wish I had done that, but I didn't have the mind-set at the time. If you have that mind-set, go for it."

—LEAH BUSQUE, FOUNDER OF TASKRABBIT

Some people dedicate their career to being an IRL fairy godmother, helping other people who want to work. Whether that's being a recruiter, a career counselor, a coach, a mentor, or an angel investor, I knew I wanted to talk to someone who, when they choose Work for their Pick Three, are really choosing to help other people in their own choosing of Work.

Leah Busque is one such person. Leah is the founder of Task-Rabbit, which helps users hire local, freelance labor to perform everyday tasks, like cleaning, moving, delivery, and handyman work. Her company was recently acquired by the IKEA Group, a company known for its particularly difficult-to-assemble furniture. In order to help people who have free time and *want* to use that time to work, Leah built TaskRabbit to help those who want to focus on their career find ways to outsource the more menial tasks of life.

She created the company when she realized that nothing like it existed to help with her own needs. Leah and her husband were on their way to meet out-of-town friends for dinner, but they were out of dog food. She knew there must be someone in her neighborhood they could hire to pick up a can of Alpo, and, as an engineer herself, she saw a gap in the market. Where was the mobile app that combined location awareness with task completion? A lightbulb went on, and Leah knew that her calling was to build a service that brought people together around helping out with tasks—providing real opportunity for people on both sides of supply and demand. She built and financed the idea for a year out of her own pocket, and then quit her job at IBM.

Leah first launched TaskRabbit as a moms' organization—because, honestly, who needs more help outsourcing tasks than moms? The moms used the TaskRabbit taskers to outsource trips to Target, grocery stores, dry-cleaning pickups—you name it! Since the mom network is so strong, the word of mouth spread like wildfire. TaskRabbit was soon expanding beyond the initial few neighborhoods Leah had launched in, and she found herself recruiting taskers to service different neighborhoods around the nation. Leah has not only built a great tech platform, she created an entirely new marketplace.

Both supply and demand were strong. On the supply side, during the tough economic crisis in 2008, there was no shortage of people willing to make money on a flexible work schedule. Even retirees who wanted to stay active found a place at Task-Rabbit, and professionals could work on nights and weekends to help make an extra buck.

On the demand side, moms, busy professionals, and those who were bedridden were all using TaskRabbit to ease the load of their day-to-day needs. One particular story that stands out for Leah is from a San Francisco mom who had a twenty-year-old son in Boston going through cancer treatment at Mass General.

PICK TWO TO CREATE ONE

Ted Eytan, M.D., is the medical director of the Kaiser Permanente Center for Total Health and vocal advocate of walking meetings. He's a family medicine specialist with a focus on total health and diversity.

In 2008, Ted posted an essay called "The Art of the Walking Meeting" on his Web site.[10] Ted says, "I was perusing through the excellent December 2007 issue of *Health Power! Prevention News* and happened on a review of this systematic analysis of the impacts of using pedometers to increase physical activity and improve health. . . . This caused me to think creatively about how to get steps in— and combining work and walking was an idea. I was hooked immediately. This is among the most contagious innovations I have ever experienced. So much so that even to this day every person I take on their first walking meeting pledges to do it again. What human would rather sit in a room and stare at someone else for a half-hour versus walk in their community?

"[I've experienced more] mental clarity and brain stimulation that comes from exercise. No ability to check your e-mail and tune out while you're walking! And there's scientific proof!

"Also, I found I had experienced the equivalent of two or three gym workouts from a day of walking meetings. Suddenly I craved them and even started looking for reasons to meet with people, if only to meet my fitness goals. To this day, I walk to and from work in Washington, D.C., two to three miles each way (different route every day), and I actually tweet about each one!"

Ted's advice on how to start your own walking meeting trend at work? "Make no assumptions. Ask people first and use their curiosity as an opportunity to learn. The thing about sitting meetings in a room is that you need have no curiosity about the other person because that's the default, lowest-common-denominator interaction. With walking, you're going to go somewhere with someone, and that requires you get to know a little bit about them—can they physically do it? Do they want to do it? What types of walks do they like? Nature or urban? What memories might this bring up for them if they've been to a place before? How will they react to things they see on the street?

"I tell the story once of an executive who I asked to go on a walking meeting with me. When I arrived at her office, she said, 'I brought running shoes to work today for my walk with you,' and to me it was the kindest display of respect and support. I will never forget that. (And then I spent the next half-hour trying to keep up with her. I will never forget that, either.) So I guess that's one meta-benefit—the relationships and special moments I've created with people that are unexpected and wonderful."

"She couldn't fly out to visit him as often as she wanted, so she went on our site, hired someone to visit him every single day, sit with him, bring him a meal, and call her every day to report on how he was doing. The tasker was another mom, and over time, the two women formed an incredible bond." Leah is honored that her company helps people redefine who their neighbors are and who they rely on. She's proud that her platform uses tech to bring people together.

If you identify as a Work Monetizer, it's wonderful that you're so passionate and driven by helping other people realize their professional goals. Congratulations on having such meaning and purpose! But, at the same time, it's easy to get too lopsided as the Work Monetizer. You're probably already a Work Passionista, and when you add onto it *other people's* Work Passionista tendencies, it can be very easy for every conversation, every interaction, every moment to turn into work.

Make sure you're taking time to be around people who aren't just looking to you for something work related. Build time into your schedule that has nothing to do with your own career or finding careers for other people.

THE PERSON WHO WRITES SUMMARIES

Just kidding! Sort of . . .

I think most of us can see ourselves in a few of these categories. While I would overall refer to myself as the Work Passionista, I've also been the Work Renovator, like when I left Facebook to start my own business. Or the Work Eliminator, like when I put that same business on hold to follow my dream of performing on Broadway. Aside from establishing lopsidedness in life, the purpose of Pick Three is to look back and see which obstacles made us stronger and how future opportunities can be tackled head-on. We are wiring our brains for a successful outcome, regardless of what may get thrown our way.

Whether you're a Passionista, an Eliminator, a Monetizer, a Renovator, a Superhero, an Expert, or some combination of several of those, there will be times in your life when you may be very lopsided toward your work. There will conversely be times in your life when family obligations or personal reasons require you to stop choosing Work and set your sights on a different trajectory.

Both Reshma Saujani and Melinda Arons were involved in political campaigns that had a different outcome than they had initially hoped. Melinda decided that after years and years of being all-in on her career and constantly picking Work, she was going to take a year off to focus on herself. Reshma channeled her energy into building a nonprofit organization to accomplish the goals of her political platform in a different way. My mother went from an intense career in medicine to deciding to be a stay-at-home mother, while Jennifer Gefsky went from a high-powered career in sports, to becoming a full-time caregiver, to launching her own start-up. Brad Takei shifted his career to support his husband, George, and Leah Busque built a business around empowering other people to pick Work.

Even in my own life, I've had moments of being all-in on my career, shifting my plans to work for a "family business," stepping away to focus on personal dreams, and eventually jumping in even deeper by starting my own business. Every single one of those decisions has come with incredible benefits and equally difficult challenges.

I'm proud of the incredible companies I've worked for, and especially all the leaders I've had the opportunity to learn from, including that dude in the hoodie. I've consistently worked hard my entire life—hopefully that will never change. What *has* changed, though, is how I work, what I want to work on, and, most important, who I want to work *for*. Somewhere along the line, I got tired of creating value for other people.

When I started Zuckerberg Media, it started off as a marketing agency and production company. Through trial and a lot of error, I realized that creating my own intellectual property sparked a fire inside of me far stronger than being in client service. I was creating all of this IP as a side hustle, including my first book, *Dot Complicated,* which is now a radio show on SiriusXM, and my children's book, *Dot.,* which is now an award-winning television show aired around the world. Or Sue's Tech Kitchen, my tech-themed family dining experience. Now Zuckerberg Media focuses almost exclusively on creating, growing, and licensing our own intellectual property. It's hard to describe how amazing it is to watch something you fully created take on a life of its own.

Now, when I choose Work in my Pick Three it comes with a slight caveat of doing work that creates value *for me*. What does work do (or not do) for you? Take note of your answer and keep a log (like the one in the back of this book). How often do you choose Work for yourself? Ask yourself *why* you choose Work. Is it because you love it, you have to, you have a deadline—what is it that moves your career? Only YOU have the power to define what your job means to you. Once you understand how, when, and why you make the choices you make, you can better figure out if changes need to be made—and how quickly you need to make them.

We all have different paths, different goals, different opinions on the role of work in our lives. Remember, as long as you balance the trade-offs that come with any lopsided decision, everything will be A-OK.

As our Work Expert MaryJo Fitzgerald says, "I believe a work-life balance is attainable from a big-picture perspective, as the demands across areas of your life and work ebb and flow. You're not going to feel perfectly balanced every day, but aim for a larger sense of balance in your week or month. Allow yourself leeway when your focus needs to be on work, and when it needs to be on other aspects of your life."

This is the essence of Pick Three.

If life sees you lopsided toward Work, that's awesome. Stop feeling guilty about the things you're not choosing and give yourself permission to kick ass in your career. If you're not choosing Work right now, you're also doing great! Whatever you choose to be lopsided in, dedicate yourself fully and do it well.

All this work talk has me exhausted. Guess that's our cue to talk about sleep!

Sleep

"Every disease that is killing us in the developed world has clear links to a lack of sleep. That's why a lack of sleep is one of the greatest health challenges we face."
—MATTHEW WALKER, SLEEP SCIENTIST

Is there anything worse than a red-eye flight? Okay, I know. There are *plenty* of worse things. I'm being overly dramatic, but if you have ever stepped off a red-eye flight and had to go straight into a situation where you had to function fully as a human being, then you know what I'm talking about. I've had way too many instances in my own career of coming straight off a flight and trying hard to look focused and alert, plying myself with way too much coffee, zoning out in meetings, and asking myself if it was really worth it. I think that each of us only has a set number of red-eye flights in us, and I've almost reached my number.

I travel like a crazy person. It's very common to see me traveling to give speeches in four different cities on four back-to-back days. A single month might take me to Kuwait, Tennessee,

Vienna, Mexico City, Texas, and everywhere in between. I have flown for more than twenty hours to be in Australia for less than twelve hours—on multiple occasions. Typically, I spend at least one night a week sleeping on an airplane instead of a bed. I'm writing this paragraph from a lounge in Seoul. I wish I could explain why I'm wired this way. It's some combination of loving what I do plus my DNA plus an addiction to the frenetic pace of life, so much so that when I'm back home for several weeks at a time, I actually start to get antsy.

Needless to say, all that travel, all those time zones, all those red-eye flights really, really, REALLY messes with my sleep. And a repeated lack of sleep takes a toll. It messes with my fitness plans (when I'm exhausted, I opt out of going to the gym and I make *terrible* decisions regarding food). It affects my memory and ability to think on my toes, and it means that when I get back home I spend a lot of time catching up on sleep when what I really want to be doing is spending time with my family.

I recently made a conscious decision to treat myself better on work trips. Here in Korea, for example, I'm speaking on a Wednesday. Randi 1.0 would have flown in Tuesday night, given the speech Wednesday, and flown back home Wednesday night. However, Randi 2.0 arrived Monday night and is staying until late Thursday. I know, a whopping two days extra doesn't sound like that big a deal, but it is to me. This schedule enables me to sleep, take care of myself, have a clear mind, and perhaps even do a bit of sightseeing. I actually got nine hours of sleep last night for the first time in, I don't know . . . *years??* I have to say I feel like a new person.

Neuroscientist Matthew Walker is the director of the Center for Human Sleep Science at the University of California,

Berkeley. He recently published his first book, *Why We Sleep: Unlocking the Power of Sleep and Dreams,* detailing the importance of getting forty winks and then some. Matthew says that becoming a sleep researcher is something you sort of fall into, but you have to practice what you preach. So he gives himself a nonnegotiable eight hours of sleep every night. I recently had Matthew on my radio show and he thoroughly shamed me for my red-eye lifestyle (rightly so), especially when he spoke about the link between heart disease and not getting enough sleep. (Not-so-fun fact: Did you know that there is a quantifiable decrease in heart attacks in the USA when we gain an hour of sleep in the fall with daylight savings? [11]) Matthew's own family has a history of cardiac disease, so he knows the importance of resting the body.

Matthew warns that we're in a global sleep loss epidemic. The average American adult is only sleeping six hours and thirty-one minutes on average. I know I've personally had less sleep than the national average several times this week. This is exactly what Matthew warns the public about. He described how it took nature millions of years to hone the eight-hour-sleep cycle. And yet it's taken us only a few hundred years to decrease that by almost two hours. Yikes.

When I commiserated with Matthew about how nice it would be if you could bank sleep—you know, sleep all weekend long and then pull several all-nighters in a row—he reminded me that sleep doesn't work that way. "You can't pay off a sleep debt. Fat cells are our credit systems. Human beings are the only species that deprive themselves of sleep for no apparent reason."

Recently, my husband and I had one of those evenings where we both collapsed into bed with exhaustion, with "Finally . . .

time for sleep" sighs, only to be jolted awake hours later by our carbon monoxide detector. You know what I'm talking about, right? That eardrum-piercing chirp that only happens when some randomly located alarm loses its battery power. Ours was located up three flights of stairs. Oy.

That stupid alarm completely ruined my productivity the next day. Honestly, I wonder what my life would be like if I could be totally functional on only four hours of sleep per night. How productive I would be! How much more I would get done! How much extra time I would have! But then I also remember Matthew telling me that I would be 4.2 times more likely to catch a cold compared to those who got more than seven hours of sleep.[12] All right, Matthew, I get it. Sleep is crucial to our health, and some people are hell-bent on promoting the benefits of catching ZZZs.

SLEEP PASSIONISTA

The person who consistently and regularly prioritizes sleep in his/her Pick Three.

> *"Slow wave sleep acts as sort of a lymphatic system for the brain. The brain shrinks a little during this phase and a special fluid rushes through and clears the waste, toxins, and stress that build up each day. That is why shift workers, who do not sleep in alignment with their natural circadian rhythms, have much higher rates of obesity, diabetes, heart disease, cancer, and other immunity issues."*
>
> **—JENNI JUNE, SLEEP CONSULTANT**

When I first thought of who in my life qualified as a Sleep Passionista, I immediately thought of my three-year-old son, who sleeps twelve to fourteen hours per day (no wonder he's so smiley!). But besides him, there's no one who truly embodies the mission of encouraging all of us to pick Sleep in our Pick Three more regularly than certified child and family sleep consultant Jenni June.

Whoa, back up now. Sleep consultant!? What is that? And how do you find one?

Similar to our Sleep Expert, Matthew Walker, Jenni found her own calling, sleep research, while helping other parents over the course of fifteen years. All before she received her specialized certifications in pediatric sleep coaching and sleep hygiene! As of today, Jenni's helped thousands of families through her own practice and at the Breathe Institute in Los Angeles. But it was when Jenni was raising her own four children under the age of six—with little to no help from her spouse, family, or caregivers—that she became obsessed with the science of sleep.

Jenni knows that discussing sleep with individuals who aren't getting enough of it is hard, emotional work. Sleep-deprived and anxious new parents recognize and respond differently to the vicious sleep cycles they've been thrust into. It's only when Jenni earns her patients' trust—and can expose them to the science of sleep—that she sees their entire paradigm of sleep begin to shift. That's when her patients' biggest, most radical transformations take place. For Jenni, this work is edifying. Simply put, sleep excites her.

I can *totally* relate to being so excited about sleep. But what happens when you can't get the American Academy of Sleep

Medicine's recommended seven hours or more a night?[13] Jenni
June says the *timing* of sleep is actually far more important than
how many hours of sleep you get. If you can correct the timing of
sleep, the hours of sleep you need will naturally be there.

"To illustrate what I mean by this, I ask my clients to consider jet lag syndrome or shift worker syndrome. If you know
someone who works at night when they should be sleeping, and
then comes home and gets all eight hours of sleep in during the
day, they still wake up a hot mess, feeling groggy and unrestored.
That is because the brain is sleeping outside of its natural biological rhythms and cannot experience the slow wave components of
sleep cycles. And no matter how many hours we get, we will not
wake up feeling truly restored."

Jenni, like Matthew Walker, practices what she preaches because, as she says, necessity is the mother of all invention. As a
sleep consultant (and Sleep Passionista), Jenni ensures she gets
her own quality forty winks by cutting out other things, like
red-eye flights, late nights out with friends or family (past nine
or ten P.M.) when she has work the next day, and no exercise
three hours before bedtime. Prioritizing sleep has only increased
the quality and therefore quantity of her work and relationships,
not detracted from it. She believes that what we actually seek is
not time, but energy—the superpower that propels us forward.
Quality sleep, Jenni says, helps us unlock limitless energy and
the cognitive flexibility to learn how to manage that energy in a
way that will enhance our relationships, daily productivity, and
creativity. This is why many of the most successful businesspeo-
ple out there extol the benefits of sleep!

So basically, counterintuitive to everything we've seen and
heard about hustling, burning the candle at both ends, working

around the clock—as Jenni's seen in her practice and as Matthew has expressed in his research and book—if you truly want to be successful in business for the long term, you have to pick Sleep.

While you may get a pat on the back from a boss for being always available and answering e-mails at 2 A.M., there is unfortunately no long-term trophy for sustained sleep deprivation. Getting enough sleep means you'll be your best self for your career, your relationships, your health, and your mood. Have you missed a few nights here and there? Have no fear, every day presents a new opportunity to Pick Three. We all have periods where getting a perfect night's sleep is unattainable. So as long as it balances out in the long run, you're doing okay.

Matthew says that since you don't know when you're sleep deprived, one night of short sleep can lead to mistakes, bad moods, and hunger pains. And that risk only increases if one has repeated sleep loss.

Which is why I was so interested to sit down with pediatric organ transplant surgeon Dr. Adam Griesemer, to find out what motivated him to go into a line of work in which he knew he would have to get very little sleep, sacrificing his own health in the process, in order to save countless lives.

PUTTING THE ZZZ'S IN AMAZZZING

Sleep is the elixir of life; the great refresher. Crucial for our health, happiness, and well-being. Yet, no matter what, we just don't get enough. Here are a few practical tips you can try out to get a great night's sleep starting tonight.

STICK TO A SCHEDULE. It's tempting to skimp on sleep during the work week, then want to binge on sleep on days off. But many experts agree that it's better to train ourselves to go to bed and wake up at roughly the same time every day. We're used to setting an alarm to wake up in the morning, why not try setting an alarm when it's time to go to bed!

DEVELOP BEDTIME RITUALS. This could be anything from a warm bath to yoga to a change in lighting to listening to a certain type of music—anything you do regularly that signals to your body, "It's time to sleep."

PUT THOSE SCREENS DOWN. The light from our devices keeps us awake. Try putting your screens down 30–60 minutes before it's time for bed. Arianna Huffington recommends, "putting your devices to sleep." Opt for a book or magazine instead. If you must be on your devices, download an app that helps reduce the blue light to something more nighttime-friendly. Or, if there's another person climbing into bed next to you, maybe consider paying some attention to them. Whatever that means to you . . .

AVOID BIG MEALS OR EXERCISING LATE AT NIGHT. Exercise is amazing for helping you sleep . . . as long as it happens at the right time of day. Like eating a big meal, exercising boosts your metabolism and keeps you awake. Ideally, you won't do either of those activities less than two to three hours before bedtime.

IS YOUR ROOM COLD ENOUGH? Many sleep experts say that the optimal temperature for getting a great night's sleep is 60–67 degrees Fahrenheit. If your room is too warm, it could affect your quality of sleep.

MAKE TOMORROW'S TO-DO LIST TONIGHT. If stress and anxiety keep you awake at night, take a few minutes before you go to bed to jot down the things you need to get done the following day. This way your brain can relax when your head hits the pillow.

SLEEP ELIMINATOR

The person who does not regularly choose Sleep for Pick Three, whether by choice due to profession, or because of life circumstances or medical condition.

"Right before you go into surgery, the family always asks, 'How did you sleep last night?' They want you to be well rested. After the surgery ends, though, they don't ask that anymore. They want you to be around and available. But forty straight hours is as much as I'm willing to do. After that, I don't think it's ethically correct to stay awake longer."

—DR. ADAM GRIESEMER,
PEDIATRIC ORGAN TRANSPLANT SURGEON

After spending a decade in Silicon Valley, where everyone works in tech, every conversation is about tech, and the Kool-Aid gets you believing the only thing that will save humanity is—you guessed it—tech, it was a pleasant surprise to meet Dr. Adam Griesemer at a friend's birthday dinner.

Sitting across the table from Adam, I apprehensively asked him what he did professionally. Worried he'd say "tech," I had to pick my jaw up off the floor after he told me he was a pediatric organ transplant surgeon and described how he routinely had to get up in the middle of the night, catch a flight to pick up an organ, and quickly head into a lengthy, complicated surgery. Here I thought I was exhausted from working in technology and the daily demands of start-up life. But Dr. Griesemer was literally sleep deprived, routinely staying awake for thirty to forty hours straight to ensure a safe pickup, delivery, and operation.

Dr. Griesemer is a quintessential Sleep Eliminator. His very important career choice does not afford him the ability to choose sleep as often as a person could, would, *or should*. What type of person can work like this? Dr. Griesemer says that while most people could train to do his job, it takes a person who is okay with sacrifice. Long gone are nights having a drink or three at social events—heck, since transplant surgeons work at all hours, social events are pretty much gone entirely. Plus, our Sleep Expert Matthew Walker warns that alcohol can fragment sleep, so if you do drink, you'll wake up more often and feel unrefreshed. Nobody wants a sleepy surgeon.

The strained lifestyle of transplant surgeons is extremely taxing on significant others as well. When you're on call, you have to drop everything, no matter where you are or what you're doing. You could be at your own anniversary dinner, or a friend's wedding, and get a call about an organ, in which case, ten times out of ten you'll be leaving your dinner date for your job. Spouses can, and often do, feel marginalized. Dr. Griesemer told me that the divorce rate in his line of work is extremely high because many spouses get fed up with feeling like a number-two priority.

Dr. Griesemer is one of the lucky ones, because his wife also works in medicine and is therefore very familiar and comfortable with this chosen lifestyle. However, that doesn't mean they haven't had to sacrifice. Adam described to me how they have chosen to put having children on hold; they both want to have children, but at the same time, both are petrified to think about bringing children into the already sleep-deprived, family-sometimes-has-to-come-second life they currently both lead. "I don't know what I'm more scared of," he admitted to me, "not having children or having them and not having time for them."

When it comes to sleep, children, and being a transplant surgeon, there is no work-life balance. There is only lopsidedness. The key is to not be *too* lopsided. Right now Dr. Griesemer feels he is well lopsided—he derives so much meaning and worth from his career that it carries him through the tough, exhausting times. He may not have children of his own yet, but he saves the lives of thousands of other children. At the same time, he acknowledges that his wife might have a slightly different opinion about his lopsidedness. While Dr. Griesemer feels he can keep going at this pace for a while longer, he doesn't always like the family sacrifices he has had to make because of his career.

So what happens when you choose a career path in which you absolutely *cannot* choose Sleep as one of your Pick Three, even if you really, really want to? Like Dr. Griesemer, many Sleep Eliminators choose to stay in motion (Dr. Griesemer told me the key: "Keep moving. Do not stop or sit down!") or they have a sofa in the office in order to take naps. They learn to love the taste of black coffee and sometimes have up to six cups a day to get their caffeine fix—though Matthew Walker advises caution here. "Caffeine and alcohol are the two most misunderstood drugs when it comes to sleep," Matthew says. "Caffeine will keep us awake, blocking the sleepiness receptors in our brains. So even if we fall asleep with caffeine swilling around our heads, we wake up so groggy, we have to have two whole cups of coffee to make us alert."

Been there, done that.

Another thing Sleep Eliminators share is that they don't want the lack-of-sleep lifestyle to last forever. Dr. Griesemer loves his career and sees it being a huge part of his life for the foreseeable future, but he also admits that eventually he wants to slow down and experience the simple pleasure of relaxing on a weekday afternoon—a luxury he hasn't been able to enjoy since before medical school.

While Dr. Griesemer loves what he does and is still challenged by his career choice, he knows he must actively balance the toll no sleep and too much work takes. When he can, Adam does yoga to help with his lower back pain, which is caused by standing for hours on end. While rare, Adam goes on vacation to places where there's no cell service so he doesn't have the mental creep of checking in or helping out on his time off. If he finds the time, he has hobbies such as fly-fishing that relax him and take his mind off his patients, who he can't always save, no matter how skilled a surgeon he may be. And he makes sure that he gets all the sleep he possibly can when he's on a plane and phones are set to airplane mode.

For Sleep Eliminators, one of the biggest questions is, what else are you choosing if you're not choosing sleep? (Picking coffee doesn't count!) Is the fact that you might be performing at a lesser capacity due to exhaustion actually worth it? If you find yourself falling into the Sleep Eliminator category more often than not, it's time for some serious introspection. Is your career literally life-or-death like Dr. Griesemer's, where you are *required* to be awake, or is it a self-imposed Sleep Elimination driven by anxiety, a toxic work culture, or a difficult boss? If this isn't just a temporary thing, and you're on a path to being a Sleep Eliminator for the foreseeable future, Dr. Griesemer has several coping mechanisms but acknowledges, "I thought it would get easier. I thought I'd have more chances to sleep or I'd get better at functioning on little sleep. It didn't and I didn't."

Every professional has an Achilles' heel, and mine is my voice. Whenever I run myself into the ground, I lose my voice and get completely hoarse, which, let's just say, is *slightly* inconvenient when you're a keynote speaker and radio host. The day of my first leading role in high school, I came down with laryngitis. At my wedding, I had it. Basically, any time I don't take care of myself, you can bet that I will be miming my words for a week or more. There was one week in 2017 when I gave four speeches on four back-to-back days in four different cities. By the final city, I was so exhausted from all those red-eye flights and time zone changes and airport sprints that I had completely lost my voice. I could barely even whisper. Luckily, the audience was lovely and understanding. It was a group of several hundred Jewish women in Philadelphia (if you're going to be under the weather, there's nowhere better to be than with three hundred Jewish moms!), and they kept bringing me tea and hot water as I did my best to squeak through my hour-long speech. One of the women, an ear, nose, and throat physician, scolded me afterward for speaking on a hoarse voice for an hour! But then she admitted that she was happy I came, rather than canceling. Unfortunately, I had to cut my favorite part out: I love to sing at the end of my speeches, but that was definitely not happening.

It took my voice much longer than normal to recover from that week, and that was a definite wake-up call to me to take my health and rest seriously. If I wanted my body to work for me, I was going to have to start doing a much better job working to care for my body. We all go through periods where we sacrifice our sleep more than we should. Sometimes, it leads to one giant wake-up call. Just ask our Sleep Renovator, Arianna Huffington.

QUICK FIXES IF YOU'RE FEELING EXHAUSTED

When you're in a bind to wake yourself up from being exhausted, consider:

A THREE-MINUTE COLD SHOWER. It sucks, it's terrible. But it will wake you up and make you feel like a million bucks, even if you got zero sleep.

GET OUTDOORS. Nothing like natural daylight to wake you up. Even five minutes outside can pep you up.

EAT PROTEIN. After a sleep-deprived evening, your body will be screaming, "Give me donuts!" But resist the urge and feed your body healthy food, or you'll just crash harder.

TAKE A MOMENT FOR MEDITATION OR DEEP BREATHING. A good power nap replacer.

SLEEP RENOVATOR

This person started to prioritize sleep more, after hitting a serious roadblock.

> *"There was no set amount [of sleep] before my wake-up call, and that was the problem. Sleep came last, or at least very far down, on my list of priorities. Getting enough sleep makes it more possible to remain centered while facing life's challenges. And it makes me more productive and more present."*
>
> **—ARIANNA HUFFINGTON, FOUNDER OF**
> ***HUFFINGTON POST* AND THRIVE GLOBAL**

Arianna Huffington is one of those incredible business moguls who, when you meet her, you just want to stay within her orbit. She's constantly reinventing herself, seeing the next huge trend years before anyone else. She's gone from politician to media figure to CEO to, now, sleep advocate. Arianna is a true example of what it is to be an advocate for women, immigrants, and taking care of yourself while simultaneously running a global business.

On April 6, 2007, Arianna collapsed from sleep deprivation and exhaustion. She broke her cheekbone and woke up in a pool of blood. That was her wake-up call. After running through a gamut of tests to find out what was wrong, the diagnosis ended up being an "acute case of burnout and sleep deprivation," or what she calls "Civilization's Disease."

We all have problems getting enough sleep, which is what prompted Arianna to launch Thrive Global after she left the *Huffington Post*. Thrive Global is a media company that uses science and storytelling to help people lead healthier lives. After her own experiences pushing herself beyond her limits, Arianna has become a leading voice and expert for self-care and sleep within the business community.

One of the many missions at Thrive Global is the creation of new role models who bust the burnout myth that the price we must pay for success is a lack of sleep. Arianna says the founder and CEO of Amazon, Jeff Bezos, not only gets the doctor-recommended eight hours of sleep, but does so because of the responsibility he feels toward his Amazon shareholders. And the former CEO of Google, Eric Schmidt, wrote a piece for Thrive about how good sleep can enhance your ability to do almost everything.

For Arianna, breaking our burnout culture is priority number one because of its economic costs. A 2016 study by the Rand Corporation found that across just five countries—the United States, Japan, Germany, the United Kingdom, and Canada—$680 billion is lost each year due to insufficient sleep.[14] Not to mention the human costs to our health, relationships, productivity, and sense of fulfillment.

Sleep researcher Matthew Walker agrees. He believes school should start later so growing bodies and brains have adequate time to fully rest. "Anytime that you try to fight biology, biology usually wins," says Matthew. And kids' bodies want to be sleeping in the early morning hours. In countries where they've pushed start times later, academic performance has improved.[15] Arianna Huffington is leading the crusade to help students by promoting better sleep.

In 2016, Arianna and the *Huffington Post* launched the #SleepRevolution College Tour at over four hundred campuses across America. #SleepRevolution partnered with major brands like Sleep Number, Marriott, and JetBlue in order to highlight the importance of sleep—particularly to students so they could cultivate better sleep habits and therefore improve their quality of life.

The #SleepRevolution College Tour was incredibly inspiring for Arianna. Her main goal was to spread sleep awareness, bring together like-minded students and organizations, and highlight all the creative ways students address the issues of stress, burnout, and sleep deprivation. The response, Arianna says, was amazing. "Students are under an unprecedented amount of pressure—from their workload to the demands and distractions of technology—but they also have an unprecedented amount of awareness about the importance of well-being and a resolve to change how we live and work." So how has the #SleepRevolution affected Arianna personally?

Arianna says she's achieved her ultimate goal: a better life! For her it's less about specific achievements than about being fully present in her own life rather than walking through it like a zombie—like she was before her collapse. Now she's still getting things done, but has a sense of joy and fulfillment that's much more easily available to tap into when she's fully recharged.

So many people choose to forgo sleep for their careers, and they're *not* staying up to save lives like Dr. Adam Griesemer. So why do we do it? Arianna believes it is related to our obsession with busyness—something technology has contributed to exponentially. With our increased pace of busywork, we're living beyond our capacity to keep up. Arianna says setting priorities and realizing how our day-to-day performance suffers when we don't prioritize sleep and well-being can help. After many years of skewing the opposite direction, Arianna is thrilled to be lopsided toward Sleep. She touts the research showing that, unless you have the genetic mutation allowing you to get by on little sleep (and only about 1 percent of the population does[16]), you need seven to nine hours of sleep—and she's happy to spread the word through her own life-changing story.

Being a Renovator means that you know that gaining energy through sleep is as important for you as it is for those around you. Maybe you've had your own wake-up call, as Arianna did, that has led you to think about work-life balance and personal health in a new way. By taking some time to refocus, reprioritize, and make sure you're taking care of yourself, you can be the very best for those around you.

One of Arianna's most important tips, if you're at a point where you need to do a bit of renovation and start picking Sleep a bit more, is to consider the role of your phone in keeping you awake. Arianna told me that her absolute favorite sleep aid is banishing her phone from her room at night. Since our phones are repositories of everything that keeps us awake—our to-do lists, our inboxes, our anxieties—she recommends putting your phone to bed *outside* your bedroom. "Doing this as a regular part of your bedtime ritual makes you more likely to wake up as fully charged as your phone."

Sleep is not a luxury, it is a necessity, and if you're at the point where you've also realized that, don't let anybody else guilt or pressure you—it's easy to fall into the trap of our culture of busyness, but it's never too late to change bad habits and renovate your life.

NAP ROOMS

The forward-thinking CEO of HubSpot, Brian Halligan, is a leading developer and marketer of software products for online marketing and sales. Brian knew that taking naps had helped his own work thrive, so he created a nap room for overtired HubSpot executives fresh off a red-eye, new parents, and exhausted employees who need a few minutes to rest tired eyes and minds.

"I've always been a fan of taking naps," he told me. "I've personally found that taking a few minutes for a nap during the day has helped me see things more clearly and given me a chance to have a better picture of what I need to work on. Some of my best ideas came during naps. And no, there aren't any time limits. Like lots of things at HubSpot, it follows our 'Use Good Judgment' policy. Nobody abuses it."

Brian is my kind of leader. "I've encouraged people at HubSpot to nap (and done it myself). We made napping at HubSpot official in September 2013 when we installed a nap room, named Van Winkle, in our Cambridge headquarters. It's been in near-constant use since. Personally, I'm a fan of the beanbag nap—there are a few near my desk. It's a great spot to catch a twenty- or thirty-minute break when I need it."

When asked what it is about napping that Brian loves so much, he says, "Put simply, napping gives me clarity. When you're a founder, you don't get a lot of free time. Some founders don't unplug at all. Napping can keep us cool, healthy, and happy in an otherwise hectic day. It can improve your perception and alertness, and even be a competitive advantage. Plus, it makes you feel great!"

The truth is, some people can hold it together when they're sleep deprived. They tackle tasks, get things done, grab bulls by horns—not me. I'm the kind of person who desperately needs to get *at least* seven hours of sleep to function, which makes it extra challenging to get the energy you need when you have a new baby and need to wake up every few hours in the middle of the night to feed. When I had each of my two sons, we were extremely fortunate that we had the resources to be able to hire a night nurse to help us during the first few weeks after they were born. The nurse arrived nightly at 9 P.M. By 8:58 P.M. I would be standing by the door eagerly awaiting her arrival. I know money doesn't buy happiness, but when it comes to having a newborn baby, money sure does buy an extra hour of sleep.

With my second son, sleep was even more difficult because I already had a toddler in school, which meant disgusting little kid germs from who knows where. Since my husband is an only child, his immunity isn't as strong as mine—I guess there's one great thing about growing up with three siblings who brought different viruses home weekly. My husband kept getting sick from the random preschool bugs brought home by our son. Here I was with a new baby, a toddler, and a husband who kept coming down with cold after cold, stomach bug after stomach bug. Somewhere around the fourth illness that entered our household within a six-week period, I got fed up with sequestering myself and our newborn from the rest of my sick family's germs. In a moment of sleepless frustration, I actually referred to my amazing husband as "dead weight" (it still makes me cringe to recall those words actually emerging from my mouth).

#UNPLUG!

Experts advise that bedrooms should be "for sleep and sex only." While that's probably not totally sustainable for the modern world (something like 90% of us sleep with our phones right next to our heads), here are a few ways to work on it:

SET A REGULAR TIME TO UNPLUG. Start off with a small "devices off" window (maybe it's one hour during dinner), and gradually expand over time. I challenge you to work up to an entire evening or even an entire weekend! (gasp!)

THINK ABOUT SOMETHING FUN, LIKE PLANNING A VACATION. Research shows simply *thinking* about going on a vacation makes you happier! Hypothetical Hawaii trip, here we come!

DO SOMETHING OLD-FASHIONED. Play a board game. Attack a jigsaw puzzle. Create an art project. Cook. Remind yourself how fun it can be to get creative, use your brain, and have real eye-contact social interaction.

PHONE JAIL. You read that correctly. If you really can't control yourself, there are devices out there that lock your phones in "prison" for an extended period of time. Shut down the Wi-Fi during certain hours or disable your access to certain apps and Web sites during time periods of your choosing.

READ *DOT COMPLICATED*. If only someone had written a book on finding a tech/life balance in our overly wired lives. . . . Oh wait, I did! But seriously, if you're struggling with this issue, you'll want to read it. #shamelessplug

The first month after a baby is born, tons of friends want to come over. They keep you company. They shower you with gifts and attention. You're running on adrenaline. You WANT to spend time with your new baby. *Sleep? What's that?* But by six weeks in, that adrenaline starts to fade. Once the fanfare ends, you're sitting on six weeks of piled-on sleep debt. Good thing a child's first introduction to the world is several months spent with their incredibly sleep-deprived parents. Remind me why we thought this was a good idea, again?

SLEEP SUPERHERO

This person becomes lopsided toward or away from Sleep to support a loved one.

"There is no such thing as sleep anymore."

—PATINA MILLER, TONY AWARD-WINNING ACTOR

It's simply amazing that after all we go through, so many of us decide to have more than one child. Even more amazing is that our partners, who witnessed the sleep-deprived hysteria, support that decision. Many of them even encourage it! It's as if there was some sort of collective memory loss of what jerks we all were on two hours of sleep. Since my boys are old enough that I've almost forgotten how incredibly sleep deprived I was, I decided for the purpose of this book to speak with a new mom, someone who's a bit closer to the experience. I had the pleasure of connecting with one of the most gorgeous, badass new moms I know to remind me what it's like!

Patina Miller is a Tony Award–winning actor and costar of CBS's political drama *Madam Secretary*. Patina gave birth to her first child in the summer of 2017, only a few months before I interviewed her for this book. "Everyone told me before about the sleep deprivation, and I was like, 'I'm a night owl, I'll be fine.' Oh, no! It's everything they warned and worse! Even when [my daughter] goes to bed, I'm still up watching her, making sure she's breathing!"

Patina told me that sleep is something she only knows by word, not action. While her mom helps out, and Patina hired a baby nurse in the beginning, it only helped her rack up a few hours of sleep. Now Patina has a love affair with cappuccinos. "I'm looking forward to her turning eighteen so I can finally sleep."

On the days Patina works, forget about it. There is no sleep. "I wake up at 5 A.M. on days we film for *Madam Secretary*. So prioritizing sleep just doesn't happen." Patina is no stranger to intense workweeks. After all, she has starred in multiple shows on Broadway and in London's West End. But having a baby is a different type of exhaustion from doing eight shows a week on Broadway, she tells me. "When I was in *Pippin* [for which Patina won a leading actress Tony Award], that was exhausting, but it was a set schedule. I knew what I had to do. It was all about me. I had time to get sleep and rest. Having a baby is *every day*. It's not like a couple of hours. Having to be there for someone who needs you 24/7 is hard work. Also, it's a human. Broadway is serious, but it's not *that* serious."

Sleep deprivation has also affected Patina's eating choices. She makes worse choices when she doesn't prioritize sleep. "I have to prepare my meals and know what I'm eating the day before. Sleep deprivation leads to bad choices."

Patina's advice to new parents is to take it one day at a time. New moms have to learn to breathe and know everything is going to be okay. "All your feelings are super valid. Be okay with the changes and the uncertainty. It's a mental and a physical change. It gets better, but it does take time. Don't judge yourself or compare yourself to other moms and other experiences." Patina advises partners to love on their wives. "We're fragile."

Has the sleep loss been worth it—the exhaustion, the craziness? Would she choose again to have a newborn during the busiest time of her career? "I would do it a thousand times over. She is the best thing that has ever happened to me. The minute we locked eyes, it's been the most amazing thing. She is the reason I do everything; she is truly the love of my life."

I got a glimpse of Patina's world. After each of my thirty performances in *Rock of Ages,* I knew I should go to bed and rest up (especially on weekends, when we did the show five times!), but I found it virtually impossible to sleep. I would be on a spotlight high—better known as actors' adrenaline.

Patina's got long hours of television production, rehearsals, memorization, PLUS a new baby who needs to feed. I'm exhausted just thinking of it all. We do what we can to survive and help those we love survive, too. Which is why we are each, in our own way, Sleep Superheroes at one point or another. How we rebuild after we fall off the sleep wagon comes from finding moments we can better prioritize sleep. And that comes with a little help from our friends . . . and Monetizers.

SLEEP MONETIZER

Someone whose current career is centered around creating a product or service that enables others to pick Sleep.

> *"Just the word 'vacation' shifts your state of mind. In today's fast pace, sometimes we long to be free of the everyday stresses and ongoing responsibilities at work and home. Stepping away allows you to replenish and hit reset so that you have a fresh state of mind upon returning to the daily routine."*
>
> **—LISA LUTOFF-PERLO, PRESIDENT AND CEO OF CELEBRITY CRUISES**

What could be more relaxing and conducive to a great night's sleep than a fabulous vacation, filled with luxurious spa treatments, gourmet restaurants, and super comfy beds, all while being rocked to sleep on the ocean? Pretty much nothing.

Combine that with the fact that you don't see too many women running huge global travel companies and I was over-the-moon delighted to have the opportunity to work with Lisa Lutoff-Perlo and Celebrity Cruises in 2015. I helped design a slate of spa services for their Canyon Ranch Spas-at-Sea that had fun, techy names like FACEialTIME, Text-icure, and Control-Alt-Relax. I had a three-month-old son at the time, so I was definitely partly designing these pampering treatments for myself!

Lisa has done an impressive job redefining and rebranding Celebrity Cruises in a crowded luxury travel marketplace. She is in the business of providing relaxing experiences for travelers, so her entire business revolves around helping other people pick Sleep as a priority when they're on her ships.

Lisa says it's no secret that a good night's sleep nourishes the mind, body, and spirit. She's a big believer personally in the mentality of "early to rest, early to rise." I asked Lisa if she practices what she preaches. "I am in bed by 8 or 8:30, and up at 5 or 5:30 every day, even the weekends, as I am one of those people that *loves* sleep. I love to sleep and truly believe that it's the only thing that rejuvenates me from head to toe."

Celebrity's Mindful Dreams program was a natural extension of the wellness programs they already had on board. Lisa was hearing from guests that sometimes it takes one to two nights to fully transition from a busy and stressful workweek or home life into a vacation mindset where there isn't any pressure to keep a schedule, make deadlines, or stay connected—unless guests choose to do so.

Lisa told me it's not so much about sleeping for the majority of your vacation. It's much more about releasing the stress that we tend to hold on to. "Vacations give you the opportunity to relax and catch up on rest and sleep without added pressures," Lisa says. "And vacations at sea are the best for catching up and changing your sleep habits. To be out on the ocean, surrounded by the sea, is the most relaxing and wonderful experience in the world, perfect for putting you in a restful state of mind."

With some solid rest, vacations help us get back to our true state of mind, so we can connect with those we love and appreciate the wonderful life we've created. "We all need to just stop and rest, but sometimes I think we need to be reminded to do so."

Lisa's team chooses treatments by staying on top of trends, getting guest feedback, and exploring what's new in the marketplace that might be interesting. "We know pretty quickly when things are working, or not, as we have guests on our ships around the world who share their experiences and feedback after every cruise. We respond quickly until we get it just right. The good news is, we get it right the vast majority of the time."

Cruises are the perfect place to relax because they pamper their guests and anticipate their needs, sometimes before guests even know what those needs are. Lisa wants her guests to come on board, unpack one time, and open their worlds. "Traveling to beautiful destinations, meeting new people, and exploring different cultures changes how we see the world. We become more tolerant, more accepting, and that tends to lead to higher satisfaction in our own lives."

Some of Lisa's favorite memories are of sailing into a port for the first time and anticipating what she'll discover that day. Those are moments we never forget, and they change us forever. You don't get that when you travel in other ways. "The connection of the sea to land is one of the things that make a cruise so special and creates a unique environment to get the best rest possible."

When asked why sleep is such a hot-button topic these days, Lisa quotes the Celebrity Cruises chairman, Richard Fain: "The fast pace of technology will never be as slow as it is today, and it will only get faster." This is true, she agrees, not only about technology, but everything. We are working harder, connected longer, doing more, and sleeping less. Jobs, children, parents, friends—we are juggling it all, all the time. "I am not sure if it says anything negative about our society, but what it does say is that we have to pay more attention to and prioritize our rest, meditation, and sleep so that we can manage the stress and recover in a healthy way. Sleep is vital for emotional and physical recovery and well-being."

As for the monetizing issue of sleep, Lisa says there's a lot of business opportunity in helping others. "People pay good money for night nannies and sleep consultants. Millions of people rely on sleep aids, noise machines, and more. And there's a reason the mattress and bedding industry is a fifteen-billion-dollar industry! [17] We've all come to the realization at some point or another that sleep is a nonnegotiable in our lives."

PICK TWO TO CREATE ONE

Sometimes making life more flexible—working from home, having a freelance job, etc.—gives us the freedom to prioritize other areas in our lives. Sara Sutton Fell is the founder and CEO of FlexJobs, the leading online service for professionals seeking telecommuting, flexible-schedule, part-time, and freelance jobs. FlexJobs offers job seekers a safe, easy, and efficient way to find professional and legitimate flexible job listings.

The bottom line is, because of remote work and flexible work options, people can better adjust and integrate their priorities in a fluid way, preempting many of the potential clashes that come from such circumstances. These options can also lead to a more healthy and sustainable life.

In a survey they conducted, FlexJobs asked people why they are interested in more flexible jobs. The survey found that since 2013, the top four reported reasons people seek flexible jobs are work-life balance (78 percent), family (49 percent), time savings (46 percent), and commute stress (45 percent). [18]

Sara believes that true balance comes from *enough* balance. For her, work-life balance is not a constant state or an end goal with a definite stopping point. In her head, the visual representation of this has always been one of her favorite childhood toys, the Bongo Board.

"To use it, the goal is to try to stay balanced in or near the middle, but inevitably, because of the way balance and our bodies work, you regularly need to have a motion of back and forth, and of having to shift more to one side and then the other, but trying not to get too far out of balance for too long so that you don't fall off. Fluidity and recovery are important. If you're doing it well, conceptually, you can stay on forever even though you're technically not always in 'perfect balance.' You just have to be *enough* in balance that it's sustainable."

If working from home or having a flexible job seems like a pipe dream, it doesn't have to be. Especially for those just entering the workforce.

Sara says that now that millennials—the largest generation currently in the workforce—have largely grown up with the mobility and flexibility that technology provides, so that they are well accustomed to communicating, learning, and collaborating online, she sees the integration of remote work happening at an even faster pace. "Millennials don't believe that work needs to be done in an office or during set hours, and they're also highly likely to seek out work-life balance and schedule flexibility, and to not approach work as the dominant priority in their lives." [19]

Being able to focus on life outside of work, while working, allows us to close in on more elusive needs (like sleep).

Another huge benefit of having a job one can do remotely is that it can make the difference between working or not working. According to a FlexJobs survey, that includes stay-at-home parents (16 percent), people who live in economically disadvantaged or rural areas (15 percent), people with disabilities or health issues (14 percent), caregivers (9 percent), and military spouses (2 percent).

So if you need to focus more on sleep (which, according to the Centers for Disease Control and Prevention, one in three American adults don't get enough of [20]), then having a flexible job can open up the world of lopsidedness you need while still earning you money to pay the bills!

According to FlexJobs, from a financial standpoint, remote workers can save an average of over forty-six hundred dollars per year and the equivalent of over eleven days per year from not commuting to work. And when looking at overall well-being, 97 percent of respondents said that a job with remote and/or flexible work would make a huge improvement or positive impact on their health and quality of life. Seventy-eight percent said that it would allow them to be healthier (eat better, exercise more, etc.), and 86 percent said they would be less stressed. [21]

MR. SANDMAN, BRING ME A DREAM!

Look, I've never freaked out and cried over something stupid when I've been well rested. I've never yelled at someone I love or snapped at a friend or coworker when I've slept well. Those have certainly all happened, though, when I haven't made sleep a priority and have lost the energy that we all need to function at our best. The times I've been at my healthiest, performing at my peak, are the times I've made an effort to prioritize sleep.

Sleep consultant Jenni June says, "When I wake up in the morning after a perfect sleep, I actually kind of smile to myself because it feels like I have the best-kept secret in the world. I feel utterly superhuman. My attitude, my drive, my body feels limitless."

This sounds strikingly similar to my perpetually happy three-year-old. Is he so cheery because he sleeps twelve hours a night PLUS a midday nap? Probably. Sleep is magical, mysterious, elusive, and crucial to being well lopsided. While some people don't need it as much as others, you can't continuously deny yourself sleep and still function at your highest level. If you neglect to pick Sleep, the effects can be detrimental to your health, personality, and emotional well-being. *MythBusters* even dedicated a special show titled "Tipsy vs. Tired" to prove that driving while sleep deprived is more dangerous than driving under the influence of alcohol.[22]

The more you know about sleep, the more sleep you'll get.

Family

"*When we experience drastic change and disruption in our lives; having a close relationship with family can help us through that.*"

—DOREEN ARCUS, RELATIONSHIP AND FAMILY EXPERT AT UMASS LOWELL

Family is wonderful, difficult, necessary, and extremely complicated. Some of us are born into a family, others create or choose our family. Whatever family means to you, the dynamics are still there—blissful, aggravating, dependable, stressful, warts and all.

Being part of the Zuckerberg family is all of the above. No matter which Pick Three I choose, Family always chooses me. That's what happens when the surname you were born to becomes a defining part of your identity. (The name Zuckerberg is German for "sugar mountain," which I guess explains my endless sweet tooth and love of dessert.) There are almost seven thousand people with the last name Zuckerberg in the world, and who would've thought that our little family (okay, not so little;

I have three siblings, and now among us we have five children) would have become the most famous of them all?

On one hand, I am so seriously lucky on so many levels. I grew up with two incredibly loving parents who are still married, love their children, and support our dreams. My parents drove for hours to attend every a cappella concert I was ever in, no matter how far away. Doing so set the precedent that, no matter what, we show up for one another. This unconditional bond has been fostered now in my own family, as my husband and I recently flew across the country for only four hours to attend my sister's thirtieth birthday party. It's followed me to different countries, like the time I left Australia for the day to attend my brother's commencement speech at Harvard University, only to turn around and fly back Down Under hours later. Mark even once left a meeting with *President Obama* early so he could catch my Broadway debut. My parents instilled in us a value that #FamilyShowsUp, and it's something I hope every single day I can instill in my own sons.

To top it all off, I feel lucky every day to have met such an incredible man, husband, and father, who continually inspires me by how much he puts our own family first in his life and goes out of his way to include both our parents in everything. He truly carries in him the same values my own family instilled in me.

And it goes without saying that I am simply lucky, blessed, honored (you name it) beyond words to have had the once-in-a-lifetime experience of being on the front lines of Facebook, being witness to my brother's meteoric rise, seeing the name Zuckerberg become synonymous with innovation and industry. To hold a name as recognized and respected as Rockefeller or Winfrey is simply amazing. Every day I still pinch myself.

It's important to have those people in your life who are there for you no matter what. As Doreen Arcus, a relationship and family expert at UMass Lowell, and our Family Expert, says, having people in your life who can support you in emotional and material ways is absolutely essential. Some people may not have a broad net they can cast to meet these needs, but they may not need as much of this kind of support as some others do. It matters what kind of person you are.

Doreen specializes in the growth of young kids and how they develop in the social context through nurture. She says that when we experience change in our lives, having a close relationship with our family can help us through a difficult transition. There needs to be somebody we can talk to who says, "I get where you're at right now."

But family is still complicated.

It's complicated to work *for* a sibling, to start. Those of you who work in your family business can relate to the toll it can take on a relationship. When one family member is the boss over another family member—when the lines blur between what's business and what's personal—things can get hairy.

In case you're sitting there sarcastically thinking, *Awww. The world's smallest violin is playing just for you, Randi,* well, don't just listen to me. I value the perspective of another woman in tech, who also shares the initials RZ and also happens to work for her brother.

Meet Ruth Zive. Ruth Zive is the vice president of marketing at Blueprint, a tech company in Canada.

"I wouldn't say the decision to join the company was difficult, but my relationship with my brother was definitely a complication. I overcame my concerns because I knew the chief marketing officer would be a buffer between us. The opportunity to be working on the inside of my brother's company was exciting to me. I know what he is capable of achieving, and I wanted to be an active part of that."

No one gets the ups and downs of working with family more than me. Okay, maybe the Jackson 5. But still, if you grow up with someone, you know them and their idiosyncrasies better than even Google does! Do you really want to work with, for, or near that person? Are you willing to sacrifice your relationship—or worse, your sanity—to see that person for more than forty hours a week and three-hundred-some days a year?

Ruth reached out to me cold over e-mail. I get thousands of messages every day from entrepreneurs all over the world on LinkedIn, Facebook, and Instagram. I wish I had the time to respond to each and every one of them! We all need that person who responds to us and believes in us. But unfortunately, there just isn't time in the day, so most of those messages go unanswered. But Ruth caught my eye. She introduced herself as a fellow woman in tech also with the initials RZ, who also works for her brother's tech company, and is also a mom (though she has five children! #supermom).

I agreed to chat with Ruth on the phone to do a smidge of mentoring. Within hours of our phone call, she had made a donation to Girls Who Code (Reshma's organization from the Work section) in my name as a thank-you for giving my time to someone who sent a cold e-mail. Wow. I've never had someone do that before, so it really made Ruth stand out in my mind. (Tip to up-and-coming entrepreneurs: do what Ruth did and nobody will ever forget you!)

Ruth has a great story. She lives in Canada, where she reports directly to her brother, the CEO of Blueprint. She told me that their relationship has evolved since they first started working together three years ago. It has strengthened because she feels appreciated as an instrumental part of helping to advance his vision. And, with a seat at the executive table, she feels empowered to interject her own voice and point of view.

I can attest that it's really cool to share such an intense experience with a sibling. I am lucky to have wonderful relationships with everyone in my family, but the experience of being on the front lines of Facebook, of seeing that company from the inside out, is something that only Mark and I share. That's what can be so cool about working alongside family; it's special and different in a way that Ruth explained perfectly: "I'm at work forty to fifty hours every week. How incredible is it that I get to share that with one of the most important people in my life?"

But what happens if you dedicate yourself a bit *too much* to your relative's passion? Ruth expressed to me that she shared her brother's passions and felt like she was making the right career move, but was definitely being hypervigilant not to lose her own identity or her own dreams in the process of working for a sibling. It sounded to me like Ruth has a very healthy working relationship with her brother.

Something I also love about Ruth is that work is only one aspect of her life. While she loves her job (and, of course, her brother), Ruth's identity is also tied up in being a mother, a wife, a friend, a practicing yogi, and a world traveler. She anticipates that one day she'll want to play more of a leading role in her career, but for now, she's comfortable being the supporting actor.

As Ruth's boss, her brother gives her a lot of freedom to chart her own course in her department. But that's not always the case.

A scenario where one sibling is the boss over another can lead to awkward power dynamics, strained relationships, and tension among other employees. It's easy to get swept away by the vision of those we care about. We want to support our family members in realizing their dreams and goals. Take Brigitte Daniel of Wilco Electronics, our Pick Three Family Passionista.

FAMILY PASSIONISTA

This person runs full throttle toward picking Family, picking it even more than most other people might!

> *"I have never regretted working for Wilco. I truly believe that working for a family business is a privilege and an honor."*
>
> **—BRIGITTE DANIEL, EXECUTIVE VICE PRESIDENT OF WILCO ELECTRONIC SYSTEMS, INC.**

Brigitte is the daughter of the founder of one of the last remaining African-American-owned private cable operators in the nation. In 1977, the same year she was born, her father founded the company with four thousand dollars, and a strong entrepreneurial spirit.He's affectionately known as Philadelphia's "Last Man Standing" within the cable industry. But the significance of a company like Wilco meant little to Brigitte when she was growing up. "At the time, I thought the cable industry was uninteresting, uncreative, and simply a way of watching television. It wasn't until I grew older that I realized the historical importance of being in an industry that determines how people communicate now and for generations to come, the sacrifices made in order to stay in business for over thirty years, and the community significance of legacy building and passing on businesses to subsequent generations."

When Brigitte matriculated at Georgetown Law School, she found herself taking up the challenges of the communications industry, just as her father had. "By the time I was twenty-one, I was vigorously pursuing communications law and the art of business practices within the telecommunications industry. The industry I once found uninteresting and mundane now held my every interest and dramatically sparked my ambitions."

Now Brigitte wakes up every day inspired that her family supports her leadership. She looks forward to continuing Wilco's legacy and leveraging her unique family business. Wilco has provided her a platform to create, to inspire, to make an impact, to be out front, and to succeed. "There is a quote that I always think of when it comes to being successful: 'If you're not at the table, you're on the menu.' Wilco has provided me a seat at the table. And it's a table normally designated for many people who do not look like me."

When Brigitte reflects on working for her family business, there's another quote that comes to mind: "Of those to whom much is given, much is required." For her this means great responsibility and hard work is what carrying on a family legacy is all about. In her ten years at Wilco, there have been many ups and downs: businesses won and lost, relationships created and ended. But overall, Brigitte takes pride in knowing what they have, what they created over four decades, what they own outright as a family.

What Brigitte loves most about working alongside her family has been the ability and the freedom to create partnerships around tech, broadband access, and the need for engagement of underrepresented communities in the tech sector. "Through my role as executive vice president of Wilco, we have been able to close digital divides, which has impacted hundreds of thousands in Philadelphia; bridge the gaps in the Philadelphia tech sector; and create on-ramps and entry points for those who have historically been left out of tech, communications, and media."

Resilience, communication, and commitment are what Brigitte thinks makes family businesses so strong. To stay, grow, and be successful as a family in business, you need all three traits. And for those considering working within the legacy of family, Brigitte says there are three other things to consider: First, make sure succession planning occurs early and is revisited often. Second, be careful of the blurred lines between the dinner table and the boardroom table. Third, maintaining a board of advisers who are not family is important to growth, accountability, and innovation.

Brigitte does find challenges working in the family business. The founder and CEO (still her father) is right down the hall, with the power to change plans on a dime, give difficult feedback, or steer the company in a direction that differs from what she might think is best. "Basically, the family business can be tricky. In the words of musician Frankie Beverly, 'It's joy and pain, it's sunshine and rain.' In other words, you take the good with the bad, as in anything, and you keep on moving. But in our case at least we keep it moving with our family. They are the people that we love and always have our interests in mind and in their hearts, and that is a great thing."

Brigitte and Ruth both agree that before you dive into working with family, just know the reality that there is much more at stake than with a nonfamily job. If things go awry, the aftermath will be a lot more complicated. You can't just chalk up contentious issues to a boss's ego. This is family; they don't get the same pass for being a jerk as someone you have little investment in. (Not saying that you should have little investment in your boss, but it's totally different when your boss makes bad or unethical decisions and your boss is, say, your DAD.)

There's also the issue of proving yourself. Both Ruth and Brigitte say there are times they have had to work harder to prove themselves in the company. Ruth talked to me about feeling pressure to demonstrate she's "deserving" of the job she has and that it wasn't just handed to her for nepotism's sake. When your merit is questioned, it can make the entire workplace uncomfortable, sometimes even hostile. Some coworkers are even afraid to interact with you, afraid you'll take things "higher up" to your relative in charge.

I totally get it. It's complicated when, no matter what you do, you're still identified and defined by another family member's success. Every day becomes a toss-up between being incredibly proud of that family member and simultaneously wishing you could go just *one freaking day* without hearing their name.

When I left Facebook, I felt like people saw me as little more than a human ATM for the first year. *A Zuckerberg? Cha-ching! Let's take her to dinner and maybe she'll open that pocketbook up! Let's sink our fingers into her and she'll introduce our charity to her brother's foundation.* But I've made my own money by working hard, and I decide how I spend it—another life lesson taught to me by, who else, my parents!

Right out of college, when I worked for Ogilvy & Mather as an assistant account executive, my mom would occasionally come visit me in New York City, and we'd go shopping. More specifically, shoe shopping. My mom would buy me expensive pairs of heels—Jimmy Choo, Stuart Weitzman, the kind I saw on *Sex and the City*. Here I was struggling, making thirty thousand dollars a year in New York City, using one of my two paychecks a month to cover rent (there was one month I couldn't afford a monthly MetroCard and had to walk everywhere— luckily I had a closet filled with designer shoes to walk in! *What?!*).

My mother's gifts didn't make sense to me at the time. She even kept the receipts so she knew I couldn't return the shoes to pay for other things like, you know, *food*. When I asked her what her deal was with buying me designer shoes in lieu of paying my rent, she said she was adamant that I make my own way and earn my living on my own. At the same time, she wanted to give me a taste of luxury so I knew what to look forward to in life, why I should work hard. She taught me to value treating myself to nice things when I'd be able to, and her lesson has stuck with me since then. It's the reason I worked so hard to become the woman I am today and why it was important for me to create the comfortable life I have for myself, my children, and my husband, without depending on anybody else to create it for me.

I know it's my own insecurity that makes me cringe every time a flight attendant says, "Zuckerberg? Are you related to . . ." or that I want to hide when a receptionist in a doctor's office calls out "Mrs. Zuckerberg!" and I feel all the other patients' eyes on me. Yet I could have changed my last name when I got married, and I didn't. I'm proud of my name and my family, and I'm proud of my own career decisions, both to go into business with a family member and then to walk away when it was time to be my own leading lady.

I CURRENTLY LIVE IN NEW YORK CITY WITH MY IMMEDIATE FAMILY, AND the rest of my family lives in California. The decision to move to the Big Apple was largely based on my love of the city, my passion for the arts, and my desire to be in the center of all the action. But part of it was also definitely seeking out my own space to carve out my path. I needed to have breathing room to focus on my husband and sons and raise our little family the way I want to, outside the scrutiny of a one-industry area like Silicon Valley. I finally have a chance to become the star of my own life story, or life theatrical show. The best part is that my family accepts, supports, and understands that need.

Family has always been a strong part of my identity. I guess when there are four siblings, you always have company, someone to play with, so I never really needed that many friends. Family was always at the core of my social life. But what if it hadn't been? Who would I be then?

When I was pregnant with my second son, I got a bit crazy. Sometimes I'm shocked that my husband still picked Family in his own Pick Three as often as he did during that time. If I were him, I would have run! There I was, crying at the diner over too-runny eggs. Screaming at his gifts of ice cream or flowers, "Do I look like a dog you just throw treats at!?" Bawling at Kodak commercials. Pregnancy is not for the thin-skinned—male or female. The weight gain, the hormone changes, the money flying out the window. I completely understand why some women just don't want to deal with it at all.

WHEN YOUR FAMILY IS FAR AWAY

More than ever before, families are geographically spread out. It's way too easy to get caught up in our busy lives and fall into the trap of out of sight, out of mind. Here are some ways to make family a priority in your Pick Three, even if they are far away.

A PRIVATE FACEBOOK GROUP. My husband and I have our own private group on Facebook where we share photos and memories. When our sons are old enough to be on social media, we'll let them join, too. That way, no matter where we are in the world, or how busy our days get, we make sure to take time for shared memories.

GROUP TEXT. Sharing your everyday, casual thoughts with your family members keeps everyone updated on one another's lives in an easy, low-touch way.

MONTHLY FAMILY BOOK CLUB. How about getting family members together over video chat once a month to all share thoughts on a book, article, or news story? Having something neutral to talk about can also relieve any weird family drama or dynamics.

SET CALENDAR REMINDERS. If you find yourself going too long without reaching out to your family, use your calendar to remind you. Schedule regular times to connect with family members. It might sound extreme to "pencil your family in," but hey, it's a modern world. (This is coming from the woman who had "Get Married" as a calendar reminder on her wedding day.)

SEND REAL MAIL. There's nothing like getting snail mail to put a smile on your face. I personally enjoy using apps that take photos from your phone and send them as postcards to people in real life.

FAMILY ELIMINATOR

The person who has made a conscious decision NOT to choose Family in their Pick Three.

> *"My decision not to get married or have kids was 100 percent my choice. I could have done either or both if I had really wanted to. But I had zero desire for children, and while I have never entirely ruled out the idea of getting married, I'm fifty-four years old and still single. . . . It's obviously not on the top of my list of things I feel I must do before I die. I just don't think I was wired to want either one."*
>
> **—ELLEN DWORSKY, WRITER AND EDITOR**

Ellen Dworsky is someone who didn't want to deal with the ups and downs of family herself. In fact, she realized when she was twelve that she didn't want to get married or have kids. How great to know exactly what you want so early! She returned home from babysitting the neighbor's baby and told her mother she was never getting married and never having kids. She was from an upper-middle-class family, and her mother worked as a nurse for most of Ellen's childhood and teenage years. Ellen's mother took care of two kids, worked sometimes full-time, sometimes part-time, depending on how she needed to be as a 1970s corporate wife to her executive husband. Even at twelve, it didn't seem like a path Ellen wanted to walk. Not wanting kids always seemed an innate part of her. Like being born with two hands. Ellen is our Family Eliminator.

Ellen had the opportunity three times in her life to get married—once at nineteen, once in her twenties, and once in her thirties. And one time she almost allowed herself to be convinced to have a baby. "But all four situations were such that it was never really going to happen. Like you say, 'I'm going to be a pilot and work for the airlines,' but all you ever do is take a couple of flying lessons. Or maybe you get your pilot's license but never look for a job. In other words, you say YES to something that you know in your heart or gut won't happen—so it's safe to say yes to the thing you never really wanted to do anyway."

Ellen has a great outlook on life. Even though she's been battling interstitial cystitis for the past six years, she's an avid reader (reading over two hundred books a year!), and she has personal creative pursuits that she actively enjoys, like making jewelry out of old buttons; making greeting cards from old ephemera, lace, and jewelry bits; and Web design. She's a professional writer and editor, and has a creative writing group that she started ten years ago that's still going strong. So when someone asks her if she has regrets, her immediate answer, before you can finish the question, is NO!

"I'm fifty-four now, done with menopause, so there's no chance I could ever have a biological child, and I've never regretted it. I do sometimes wonder what will happen when I'm old, unmarried, and childless, but there's no guarantee that I wouldn't end up divorced or that my husband wouldn't die before me—or that I'd be the one taking care of him and adult children. And there's no guarantee that a kid is going to take care of you in your old age. I know plenty of adult children who want nothing to do with their parents."

It was just so clear to Ellen that she didn't want to marry and have kids that she never questioned her lack of desire and never felt like it was some sort of issue she had to get over, either. Her absent biological clock made her choice easy, and she never worried about what other people thought of her decision—though there was a time when she *claimed* she was waiting until thirty-five to get married. But that was more a way to end the conversation when people asked than anything else. Unconsciously, she didn't feel entirely free (as an adult) to repeat what she said to her mother at only twelve years old.

"I looked down that path and said, 'Nope, that's not my path. I'll make my own.' It's not as if I had any real-life examples to look at, so I blazed my own trail. . . . Don't worry about what other people think of you and what you should do. Do what's best for you."

I truly admire Ellen for knowing what she wanted, but the truth is that there are many women out there who just don't know whether they want kids, or aren't ready, or feel like they are running out of time. I have many friends who have gone through difficult IVF treatments. I've sat with friends going through the painful process of freezing their eggs, and the weeks of shots, treatments, and recovery, just for the option of extending their choices and decision time line. I've had friends go through devastating miscarriages—some of them as late as the final weeks of pregnancy. Everyone has their own journey when it comes to family, and for some, that journey is more difficult, stressful, or even brutal than others.

And it's not just women, or women who haven't had a child. My business partner and his husband had miracle twins via surrogate after multiple very disappointing miscarriages and failed attempts by their egg donor.

Even in my own family, I know that my husband, who's an

only child and never had any siblings, would love to have a bigger family. He'd love if we had a third child! But for me? I'm undecided. I have a busy career. I have two beautiful children. What if we have a third child and it messes all that up? But what if I don't have a third and I wind up regretting that decision and wishing that I had? The problem is that I don't really have the luxury of time to be undecided. Whether you have zero children or ten children, or you're on your fourth marriage, or it's just you—the pressure to make decisions never ends.

I know I'm incredibly lucky and privileged that I even have a choice. And the beauty is that for every woman in this situation, every single choice is valid. Choosing NOT to have a third, or second, or any children, is just as important as choosing to have a child. Sometimes there are many situations beyond our control, beyond comprehension, that force us to make difficult decisions in picking Family as one of our Pick Three. And sometimes we just know that it's not right for us. *(But just in case I ever do have that third child, you—the third—were never a bad decision or a drain on my time. Love you!)*

So what happens when all of that is taken away in one fell swoop? That's what happened to Rebecca Soffer, an only child who considered family core to her identity. Rebecca found herself alone after losing her grandmother; then her mother, who she considered her very best friend, suddenly in a car accident; and finally her father, to a heart attack a few years later. What happens when you desperately *want* to pick Family in your Pick Three and you simply CAN'T? This is how life has played out for Rebecca.

WE ARE FAMILY . . . BUT WE'RE FIGHTING RIGHT NOW.

Family conflict is real. If you're in the middle of family drama right now, here are a few things to think about:

WRITE IT DOWN. Sometimes writing things down can help you articulate your feelings better so you can deal with your emotions.

BRING IN A NEUTRAL THIRD PARTY TO HELP WITH A DISCUSSION. Maybe it's a friend, a faith-based community leader, a neighbor, or an official mediator, but having a neutral third party lead a discussion will help keep people reasonable, rational, and open to hearing other viewpoints.

TALK TO A PROFESSIONAL. Whether it's a therapist, an online support group, or countless other resources, it can often be helpful to hash out your feelings with someone who isn't personally invested in your family.

HOST FAMILY GATHERINGS IN NEUTRAL TERRITORY. Perhaps Thanksgiving dinner is best at a restaurant instead of at somebody's home? Having other guests present or activities planned can be helpful and can give everyone some common grounds for discussion.

FAMILY RENOVATOR

The person who hits a serious roadblock in their life that forces them to refocus and reconsider how they define and pick Family.

> *"My darkest moment was when I realized, 'I don't have a home anymore. There's no one expecting me for Thanksgiving.' I said this to the rabbi at my dad's funeral and he said, 'You're right. You have to create a new foundation. I don't want to sugarcoat it. You have to do it. Figure out what your new foundation can be and build it.' That was the best advice I got."*
>
> **—REBECCA SOFFER, FOUNDER OF MODERN LOSS**

After losing both of her parents in her early thirties, single, without kids, Rebecca was able to completely renovate and adjust her life to now helping thousands of people who are going through similarly difficult experiences. It wasn't something she grew up wanting to do. She wasn't a little girl dreaming about creating a Web site dedicated to losing people you love. Her goal was to become a journalist. She worked at *The Colbert Report* for several years, but while she was there, she lost her grandmother and her mother, and her entire world was completely thrown off its axis.

Rebecca started having awful PTSD. As an only child, her father was all she had left of her family, and she grew terrified of something happening to him. She would often drive hours to check on him. When her worst nightmare came true, and he passed away, "I thought my life was over," she told me through tears. "I truly believed there was nothing left for me." At the age of thirty-four, Rebecca had become an orphan. She felt untethered from everything she'd known. She had always been the kind of person who made sure to pick Family. "My identity was shattered. I was like, 'I'm a parent person. I'm a family person,' then all of a sudden I didn't have any of those things."

Rebecca was using every atom in her body not to have a complete meltdown. She had to pretend she was okay to pitch funny stories at work. She felt like she was acting. "I had a lot of trouble finding people I could connect with to talk about this with. People would ask, 'How are you?' but I didn't want to be honest over the water cooler about what a mess I was. I have a lot of friends, but they didn't know what to do for me."

For a while Rebecca found herself turning down invitations to events that seemed too painful to stomach. She told me how difficult it was to look at her social media accounts on Mother's Day and Father's Day only to see people's smiling pictures with their parents. "Many years went by and I was very resentful of people who had living parents. I said 'no' to a couple of wedding invites because I didn't want to see a dad walk someone down the aisle. On Mother's Day I'd go to the park and read a book."

Today Rebecca has rebuilt her own family, with a husband and two adorable children. She truly inspired me during our discussion and taught me that every situation—no matter how difficult—can be rebuilt from the ashes, reconstructed, renovated. "You find your family. My parents were my best friends. I miss them every day of my life. I still find myself in situations where I say, 'I should call my dad and tell him that. Oh, wait, I can't.' They never met my children, which is really difficult for me. I am still a parent person, so I find other people's parents I connect with. I've made a real effort."

Now, through the Web site she started, Modern Loss, Rebecca works on helping others feel comfortable and free to share how they feel when dealing with loss. Death is still a taboo topic in society. It's considered a downer to talk about it. "This is definitely going to happen to you. It happens to everyone. You are going to lose somebody you love at some point. What Modern Loss wants is to address it now and help society normalize this conversation. We wouldn't be doing this if it didn't happen to us. It stems from personal traumatic experiences."

It might sound like a bummer to write about death all day, but when you meet Rebecca, she is about as far from a bummer as anyone you'll ever meet. A ball of sunshine and optimism, Rebecca has a huge, friendly smile, a bright, cheerful attitude, and warm, welcoming eyes. "I don't think Modern Loss is a site about death. It's a site about life. It's about resilience and optimism. It's about the person left behind and what happens after that."

If you can relate, my biggest takeaway from speaking to Rebecca is that you can still pick Family even if, by traditional standards, you don't have one. Rebecca never stopped considering herself a family person, she never stopped picking Family, she just redefined what family meant in her life. When she didn't have one, she built one with her company and the Modern Loss community. And ultimately, she created a new one with her husband and children.

Maybe you're picking up this book in the throes of a difficult situation that has forced you to refocus and reprioritize.

If you feel like you'll never figure it out, that you'll never be able to get past the hurt to Pick Three things on your own again, take Rebecca's sage wisdom. "I thought I would be sad every minute of every day for the rest of my life. You need to see the forest through the trees, and the only way you can do that is taking tiny microsteps forward—and probably a million steps back. And yet, when it ebbs and flows along with that tide, a lot of good stuff gets washed onto the shore. For me that was a partner in the Web site and my husband. I feel like my mother sent him to me. And my kids—I never thought I'd have them. I'm not going to say when or how it will happen, but it will get better."

If you've had similar experiences to Rebecca in losing your family, I hope you have a way to renovate your life as well (and that you'll go to Modern Loss for some support). There are so many ways to extend our family beyond our blood and DNA. We can cultivate great friends and create new families—as Rebecca did with her own.

We can even choose a career where Family is prioritized so much that your coworkers become like blood relatives. But sometimes in the workplace, family isn't as highly regarded as it should be. The United States is the only developed country in the world that doesn't have guaranteed maternity or bereavement leave.[23] And some companies don't prioritize family at all, punishing, even firing parents who have to leave work for family emergencies.

HOW TO HANDLE A BOSS THAT DOESN'T WANT YOU TO PICK FAMILY

Work and family often collide, which can lead to rising stress levels and frustrated spouses. In an Alamo Rent A Car Family Vacation Survey, around half of American workers reported feeling "vacation shamed," or feeling guilty for planning and taking a vacation. Because of this, the survey reports the quality of family vacations is being conversely affected. Forty-nine percent of American workers believe the most important benefit of traveling together as a family is spending quality time together, yet nearly two-thirds of working families say they spend time working while on family vacations, with half saying it's because they don't want to come back to a mountain of work. More moms reported this feeling than dads (52 percent vs. 38 percent). And to top it all off, more than one in five U.S. workers say they are expected to check in, even though most (53 percent) prefer to unplug from work while on family vacations.[24]

So what can you do about getting in quality family time when you have a difficult boss? Julie Cohen is an executive coach and the founder and CEO of Work. Life. Leader.—a yearlong program for those who want to transform professionally. She's a work and lifestyle expert who advises clients on everything from the pros and cons of changing surnames after marriage to job searching while pregnant. She says handling a boss is both tricky and important. "When a boss's expectations are infringing on your personal life or family time, it's better to address it sooner than later, because ignoring it means the boss assumes there's simply no problem. And constant frustration, anger, exhaustion, or upset does not allow anyone to operate at their best."

Right! So how can we talk to our boss about it without pissing them off? "Often one conversation expressing concerns about the impact of the boss's style/expectations can raise awareness and stop or at least lessen the undesired impact.

"To raise this awareness, request some time with your boss to talk about delivering the best results for the company/ organization and explain the way you work best. Focus on mutually desired results (high-quality product, creative ideas, thorough analysis, etc.) and explain how you best do this. You can state your preferences and also show that you can be flexible, too . . . yet your best work is done in a specific time window."

Sometimes a boss may not care, though, and then you're back to square one. But having the conversation is still a good place to start. "If you don't have the conversation, you'll never be in a position to come up with a better situation. Ideally you want to get to a place where your boss is clear on the best way you work; and you can communicate with him or her if and when you need something different than they are providing."

Okay, but I'm reading this book from the white sands of Bora Bora and my boss has texted and called me twenty times. I need them to understand my boundaries NOW. Help! "Another, more covert way to address off-time requests is to ignore them until you are on the clock, or working at a better time based on your preferences. You can test this once or twice and see what happens. Some bosses may send messages and communicate requests at off-hours because that's when they work, and they may not necessarily expect a response until the next morning, just as colleagues in global time zones will send messages and requests when they are working but likely would not expect a response until an appropriate time in your time zone. You can experiment with applying that approach with your boss. If it's a problem, they will tell you. If it's not, you'll see that you have more autonomy than you thought."

For those dealing with a boss who's cutting into family time, follow Julie's plan of attack:

"First, assess what impact your boss's behavior is having on you and your ability to do your work well. Once you're clear on this, talk to the boss to attempt to address the problem directly. You will always want to make it 'about the business' and frame your concern with improving your ability to do your job more effectively.

"Second, be specific to explain what's not working. Besides having a conversation, it's good to document your concerns while they are happening and save any e-mails or voice mails related to your concerns. Ideally you want to work with your boss to remedy your concern as opposed to making your boss the 'bad guy.'

"Third, if the 'bad behavior' is not something that you are comfortable addressing on your own, seek out someone else, possibly another organizational leader, or a human resources professional, to assist. Of course, if the behavior is harmful to you or others, or illegal, remove yourself from the situation and seek assistance when you are in a safe environment."

To summarize, Julie says, "'Enough is enough' is very personal depending on what you want and need from your work. One equation to consider is when stress, frustration, and/or upset from work become greater than the benefit (money, enjoyment, and accomplishment, to name a few) you experience. This barometer is values based, so each person needs to decide what they are and are not willing to attempt to manage with a difficult boss."

If you have a boss who just consistently does not respect your need for family time, you have two choices about what to do— stay and tough it out or, if it's available to you, find a different job elsewhere. However, when it comes to family, you don't always have a choice, especially when a child is sick or injured. I remember getting off a long overnight flight, turning on my phone, and hearing a voice mail saying, "Your son's been admitted to the emergency room. COME NOW." (Luckily everything turned out okay.) "It's a rite of passage," several mom friends told me. But sometimes parenting can be flipped on its ear so it unexpectedly turns into a full-time focus.

IT TAKES A VILLAGE

Sometimes when life throws us for a loop we're tempted to throw on a superhero cape and solve everything ourselves. But whether it's the family you're born into, the family you've created, or the family of community, those around you are eager to help . . . if you let them. Here are a few ideas to help you lean on your support network a bit more.

TELL PEOPLE HOW TO HELP. A new baby, a move across the country, coping with illness, unexpected grief—you name it, people want to help. They just might not know how. Do you want people to bring meals or help with grocery shopping? Do you need help caring for a loved one? Are there specific items you need? Give people tangible ways to help you get the support you deserve.

SEPARATE THE HELPERS FROM THE ENABLERS. Whether you're recovering from addiction, focusing on getting healthier, or trying to live a happier, better life, lean on those around you for help. Join a support group to find common ground with others going through the same thing. Tell your loved ones how they can support your journey and things to avoid saying so as not to derail your progress. Identify toxic people in your life who aren't supporting you and figure out how to love them from a distance.

HIRING PEOPLE. It's great to have family around when you have a new baby, but it can be difficult to give a family member feedback or ask them to do something differently. It's nice to have a roommate who cooks, but not if they're constantly making unhealthy food that is setting you back from your goals. Figure out if there are areas of your life that are causing you stress and creating conflict in your relationships with your loved ones. Then, figure out if it might be realistic for you to muster up the budget to bring in professional help instead. Sometimes saving your relationships with friends or family members is worth coughing up a bit of extra money.

FAMILY SUPERHERO

This person becomes lopsided toward Family to support a
loved one.

> *"Do I regret my decision to prioritize my son? NO. But I
> admit there are days and moments when I definitely miss
> that 'me' at work. At some point, all mothers face this
> crossroad in parenting. It was the same for me. I tried to
> prioritize what was important at that time in my life. The
> rationale was that I could always go back to having a paid
> career at any time in life. The bank wasn't going to miss me.
> Career could wait. But my son needed me by his side—as
> his mother, as a mentor, as a friend, as his anchor."*
>
> **—RAMYA KUMAR, AUTISM ADVOCATE, MOTHER**

Sadly, for some, the emergency room is not just a one-day thing.
While a few situations have rocked my world for forty-eight
hours, tops, some parents have to make difficult decisions and
choose to upend their lives permanently to accommodate the
needs of their family. Take, for example, Ramya Kumar, who had
been a professional banker since the day she graduated with an
M.B.A. from business school. Hungry for success and climbing
the corporate ladder at breakneck speed, Ramya had just been
offered a vice president position at the multinational bank she
was working at when her autistic son suffered a setback and his
therapist recommended that Ramya spend more time with him
if possible, especially since he was responding so well to their
unique, strong connection.

Ramya's husband took on most of the family's economic responsibilities as she reduced her working hours for four years,
juggling work, her personal life, and constant trips to differ-

ent therapists and hospitals, then realized that she wasn't able to give 100 percent to either work or her son. She reevaluated her priorities—work or son—and her heart knew which one to choose. She left the workforce and dedicated herself to taking care of her son 24/7.

Choosing to stay at home and take care of her son was a difficult decision both financially and personally. Letting go of a career that had formed a part of who Ramya was for so long, that earned her respect and gave her individuality, was hard. But her son's needs outweighed everything. While she feels fulfilled with what she has achieved in life and happy with the decisions she's made thus far, she admits to a bit of an ongoing struggle in her mind. "I have learned that my identity is who I believe in my head I am. In fact, my identity is actually evolving all the time. Having said that, when I think about what defines me in this world more than anything else, it has to be my son."

The decision to be a Family Superhero is not without its own day-to-day challenges. Ramya still struggles with her self-worth. She feels that every day she has to be productive to prove her worth and value to herself. Sometimes, she ends up overstretching and pushing herself too hard, which leads to anxiety and stress—more so than when she was doing paid work. She has to navigate through her own disappointment and frustration and often not only feels guilty, but also questions her own abilities. "With this choice, the risk of feeling lonely and socially isolated is very high. You might long for a grown-up conversation to keep your sanity. You might feel left behind as the world seems to be overtaking you. You feel inferior sometimes! The world seems to be a much scarier place."

It's a scary place for many reasons, Ramya says. First, when you choose family as a career, you're living an around-the-clock job, working overtime even on holidays and vacations. And with the most difficult, hard-to-please boss to boot! Plus, the world around you treats you differently.

"You're suddenly made to feel not savvy enough for modern society—stereotyped! Those of us who have decided to give up our careers to raise a child are ridiculed. This role of being a career homemaker is degraded and no longer viewed as an admirable pursuit. Doesn't do much for our already dwindling self-esteem!"

Ramya refers to her son as her "guru" because he has given her an absolute philosophical insight into life. "People go on a journey of finding purpose to their life, seeking the meaning in books and spiritual gurus. My guru lives with me. I just have to understand his ways of teaching. He taught me silently that I am not perfect. I cannot change the unchangeable, I can't always have it my way, I have to learn to be patient, and I have to see light even when it is so dark around."

If Ramya weren't taking care of her son she would still be in pursuit of social status, running the corporate rat race, but being with her son has given her a new perspective on life. It's taught her to stop and look closely at every little detail, and be amazed at its beauty. She happily lives life for the moment and appreciates the little things. Her son has taught her that the most valuable thing in life is . . . her son.

But it's not all about sacrifice. Being a Family Superhero can be fun! Ramya says you get a golden opportunity to relive your own childhood while becoming your child's best friend. She recommends jumping into puddles, joining your child in their joy, and sharing with them the things you did as a child yourself. You get to live your childhood once again—your biggest reward. "Let your child lead you into their magical world, experience it with them. It's a true chance to let go of your inhibitions, look at life through the eyes of your child. Believe me, you will suddenly see a whole new meaning to life and your outlook toward everything will change."

It's important to note that women are not the only parents who lean toward sacrifice. Ramya says both parents tend to have the same family, life, and career aspirations to start with. But how life actually gets played out is usually different, due to personal situations, financial demands, support systems available, and numerous other variables at play. "Since mothers are usually viewed as the primary caregivers in most cases around the world, they slip into the caregiver role very easily and in most cases willingly."

While it's very common that women do end up "paying the mommy penalty" at work, this remains a very personal decision that differs from family to family, depending on each unique circumstance. "Everyone, in general, invests their time and emotional energy according to their own priorities. In a majority of cases, including mine, the current situation called for me to be [my son's] support and his anchor, a role I happily took up for myself. This decision was mine. Therefore the word 'sacrifice' does not fit in."

While Ramya says it was not a sacrifice for her, she acknowledges the many parents who do sacrifice for their families. Many working parents choose to accommodate their children's needs at the expense of their career path, and many more are forced to choose work over parenting or vice versa due to their finances, not their free will.

What's crystal clear, though, is that Ramya is certain she made the right decision for her family, her career, her life. "It was a difficult decision, but I would it do it all over again in a heartbeat, because it was the right thing to do for me and for my son."

I know this story is familiar to many people, for all sorts of reasons. When you have a family, you have people who depend on you, and those people have needs and get immersed in situations and events that are outside anyone's control or ability to predict. You just find yourself leaping into animal-instinct protector mode. Sometimes we are lucky and the crisis is short-term. But I have spoken to so many parents who have had to step away from a career they loved, move to a new place, find a different school, become an advocate to fight for better medical care—suddenly having a massive new life priority that they never, ever saw coming. If you are the Superhero of your family, my one question back to you is, Do you have a Superhero of your own? Who prioritizes and takes care of you, if you're so busy prioritizing and taking care of others?

I'm not currently at a place where I would choose to stay with my sons all day, every day, but that doesn't mean I'll always feel this way, or that I wouldn't change my mind at the drop of a hat if a situation arose where I felt I needed to be there. I have extreme admiration for parents who do choose to stay at home and pick Family first, every single day.

The one thing that I know all parents are thankful for, whether we are at home or work, or live at airports, or what have you, is that we are grateful for the smart, incredible, thoughtful people who work in children's entertainment.

FAMILY MONETIZER

Someone whose current career and mission is around creating products for families!

> *"This generation is growing up with terrorism as a daily aspect of their lives. Kids are highly aware of what is going on politically and globally. When first graders are having lockdown drills in school, we need to arm them with superheroes to make them feel powerful, provide content to help them with resiliency, and put on shows to make them feel safe. This is on my mind all the time right now."*
>
> **—HALLE STANFORD, PRESIDENT OF TELEVISION AT THE JIM HENSON COMPANY**

Helping other people pick Family has been a longtime profession of Halle Stanford. Halle grew up with a single mom and watched a lot of television. She loved TV, especially kids' TV. The stories and characters kept her company when she felt alone. And the older Halle grew, still addicted to watching *The Smurfs* even in high school, the more she wanted to create things for kids that made them feel the way some shows made her feel. She imagined herself as a mother, telling stories on television. Fast foward to now—she is president of television at the Jim Henson Company, where she develops content to bring families closer together. And where I'm lucky enough to get to work alongside her as co–executive producers on *Dot*.

At Henson, Halle realized she was mothering hundreds of thousands of children through her television programming. The stories she creates spark ideas in young kids, helping them find their passion. Families watch these stories together, creating new memories. Each show gives a toolbox of opportunity to families, opening up new worlds for children. "Maybe you don't live by the ocean, but then you watch a show about fish and suddenly feel inspired to learn more."

Kids have the best imagination and because they learn so much all at once, it's fun for Halle to design new shows around each new generation of preschoolers. For her, it's an exciting challenge to find stories that can touch each member of the household. And right now is the best time to inspire people to be more courageous and creative. "We're always pushing ourselves to develop excellent stories. We have a lot of fun. There's a lot of glitter and unicorn horns and goblins."

Many of the children of Henson employees have grown up on the lot. Some babies from when Halle first started are now graduating high school. There's a wonderful culture of parents involving their own families in the experiences they create and produce. "When we want to test something, like if teenagers want puppet shows, we get to use our own kids when shooting pilots. They are a part of the community."

Halle brings parenting and kids into everything she does, thinking about what they need and how to apply that in programming. "I developed a show a while ago around how my little boy loved to dance. I thought, *Wow, we really stereotype dance for girls,* so we developed *Animal Jam.* I love watching TV with my oldest son in order to do research."

Halle says she was drawn to producing our show *Dot.* because it prepares kids to live in the modern age and be good digital citizens, something that's on every parent's mind. "I feel like parents want to know how their kids can live in this world. They're worried about the future, we see limited resources, we see potentially scary times ahead, so how do we get kids understanding and empathizing? How do you keep kids innocent and in the age group they are supposed to be in? We don't need to open their eyes—their eyes are wide open."

I am especially grateful to be working with Halle on *Dot.* because I feel like creating work that includes my children is a secret life hack of sorts. When I wrote the original book *Dot.*, which our award-winning TV show is based on, about a tech-savvy girl and her adventures, my firstborn was first and foremost on my mind. Later, when I went on a *Dot.* book tour, my son would sit beside me and read the story aloud with me, making my work all the more enjoyable and meaningful.

At the launch party for the show, both my sons got to be a part of Mommy's work. And I could feel the pride radiating off my eldest when I gave a speech thanking him for his companionship in Dot's (and my) journeys.

Now my sons show off Dot as if she were their two-dimensional sister and claim my latest children's book, *Missy President,* as their current favorite book.

My boys have joined me at many work events from filming commercials (yay college fund!) to the launch of my family-friendly, tech-themed café, Sue's Tech Kitchen—and I wouldn't have it any other way. There's no feeling quite like seeing your children take pride in your work, really understanding what you do. My sons' teachers tell me that anytime they get to pick a book at school, they both choose *Dot.* and exclaim to their class, "That's my mama's book!" There's nothing that quite matches that feeling. So thank you, Halle!

The one thing I can see is that when your work and family blend together so seamlessly, it can sometimes become difficult to separate them. Sometimes my son doesn't want to go *work* at Sue's Tech Kitchen with me, he just wants to spend some time with his mom. Sometimes I need to have an adult conversation that doesn't revolve entirely around what nine-year-old Dot would say. And Halle and I had a good laugh about how some people in the children's entertainment space can take their job so seriously that they forget to just stand back, smile, and appreciate what they are building and creating. So, if you're a Family Monetizer in any way, just make sure you're getting the healthy separation you need.

With leaders like Halle at the helm, I couldn't be more thrilled with the future of children's entertainment.

SEEKING FAMILY THROUGH COMMUNITY

Family is not just designated to those who share your DNA. Blended families, mixed families, adopted families, and spiritual families are just some of the types of familial love we can experience.

Sometimes the traditional family unit is just too complicated, toxic, or completely nonexistent, leading people to seek out an alternative community that can fill the place of a family. In these circumstances, many people turn to spiritual or religious communities.

William Vanderbloemen is the CEO and president of the Vanderbloemen Search Group, a pastor search firm that helps churches and ministries build great teams. I asked William if he believed that religious communities can fill a need for those who are looking to find their family elsewhere. He told me that religious institutions can absolutely take the place of family.

"There are lots of reasons people turn to religious institutions. Sometimes it's an event for a child, a big holiday, a moment of crisis, or a friend reaching out and inviting them. But the reason they stay is almost always the relationships they develop there." William acknowledged that after working with thousands of religious groups, he has seen congregations of unrelated people become much closer than a lot of families he knows.

Remember, what you define as family doesn't have to be the family you were born into. It can be the family you create, or the community you surround yourself with that supports you and aligns with your beliefs. If you're not getting fulfillment from your traditional family unit, try seeking out other communities, such as a religious or spiritual community, that can fill the void and help provide a sense of belonging.

That's why William considers his work so important. When he is tasked with hiring a pastor, he feels like he is hiring family, because that's what this leader will be to so many people in the community. "Over the last few years, we have spent a lot of time and money trying to learn how to interview a whole family for a job." Even though his clients are hiring for one position, William finds it crucial that the entire family comes to the table ready to serve the community with love and faith.

WE ARE FAMILY

I wish I could give you great advice about how to be parent of the year or even child of the year while also focusing on your career, but I'm far from being the perfect parent or daughter or sister. The honest answer is that on the days I pick family, I do a great job. I call my mom and have good conversations. I FaceTime my ninety-three-year-old grandma. I prioritize spending quality time with my children. I show up, both mentally and physically. But I also have a busy career, so I don't choose Family every day in my Pick Three. I'm not the mom who picks up at school every day and has dinner on the table at 6 P.M. I'm not the sister who calls my siblings every week. (I see everything they do on social media anyway!) Maybe you'd prioritize differently, and that's totally fine! It's why I'm writing this book—we *all* prioritize differently. There should be no judgment about who does what why, when, or how. Only that they do it at all.

Just last week, I showed up to pick up my son from his afterschool activities. School pickup has a protocol: "Raise your hand if you're picking up from basketball." Half the hands go up in the air. "Raise your hand if you're picking up from chess." A different set of hands go up. Then there's "Raise your hand if you don't remember which activity your son does and you're just grateful to be here." One solitary hand goes up: MINE. (In case you were wondering, it was basketball. World's Okayest Mom right here, folks.)

Many days, I'm full of guilt. Other days, I can laugh about it. I like to say that I'm a professional techie and an amateur mom, but in all honesty I have absolutely no idea what I'm doing. Being a mother is the toughest, longest-running start-up I've ever launched. Each day brings a new entrepreneurial pivot.

Everyone has their own reasons for choosing or not choosing Family. In fact, the very word *family* means different things to different people. Whether you prioritize the family you were born into, the family you've assembled from people around you, the family you've created, or a family of spiritual or community purposes, we all define the word *family* differently. What you want out of family ten years from now may look very different from what you want right now, and you know what? It's all great. If you're not prioritizing family right now, don't feel guilty and don't let anybody else project their values onto you. If you are prioritizing family, that's excellent, too, whatever that family looks like for you. And if you are in a difficult time because life has dealt you an unexpected family-related circumstance, know that you are far from alone. Humans all seek belonging because, as humans, we *need* to belong. Belonging to each other, to our friends, to our families, and to our respective cultures, society, country, and planet.

Belonging is fundamental to happiness and well-being. One study from the journal *Science* shows that social connection strengthens our immune system, helps us recover from disease faster, and may even lengthen our life.[25] People who feel more connected to others have lower rates of anxiety and depression. So regardless of what family means to you, we all have a lot more in common on this topic than you probably think.

Fitness

"*A purpose, a plan, and accountability, that's what it takes to make fitness a lifestyle.*"

—TONY HORTON, MOTIVATIONAL SPEAKER, HEALTH AND WELLNESS EXPERT, CREATOR OF P90X

Fitness means different things to different people. Fitness, as I am calling it, means anything related to physical and emotional health. Many times, the two go hand in hand and I experienced this while training for a marathon. Halfway through my senior year in college it felt like everyone had jobs lined up after graduation—everyone except me. See, I wasn't going the typical route of management consulting, investment banking, medical school, or law school. Nope, I wanted a job at a marketing or advertising agency—jobs that don't typically recruit months in advance—so I had been totally left out of the on-campus recruiting process that began long before graduation. While my senior year of college was one of the most fun years of my life, I couldn't help but feel a bit of uncertainty about where my future was heading. In high school, I knew what lay ahead as long as I got good grades, studied hard, and got into the best college possible. But once you graduate from college, the future becomes an endless cycle of anticipation and uncertainty.

I started networking like crazy, applying for every marketing job possible, calling and e-mailing any fellow Harvard alumns who worked in advertising. But it was all the same story: *Any open job would need to be filled immediately. If you aren't able to start work within two weeks, please talk to us again after graduation. K thx bye.*

To get myself out of my funk, I decided that if I was going to be the only Harvard graduate without a job lined up then I was going to pick another goal I could work toward and feel proud of. So after a long night of cheap box wine and Thai food with my friend Susan, we both decided to register for the Chicago Marathon.

When you've never really run before, training for a marathon sounds like a fun challenge. The beginning was painful, bloody, hell. I had no idea what it was like to go on an eighteen-mile run, lose a toenail, or be doubled over on the side of the road after hitting the proverbial "wall." But I had set my goal, and I stuck with it. Much to my surprise, I saw rapid progress. I was getting stronger as my mileage increased. I was twenty-one years old and suddenly I felt like I had a higher purpose I was working toward—employed or not.

The Chicago Marathon takes place in early October, so I figured I would spend the summer training (and, ahem, living with my parents), run the marathon, and afterward focus on getting a job. But, as the saying goes, the best-laid plans of mice and women yadda yadda yadda . . . so of course, a mere days before graduation, that's when I got that call from Ogilvy & Mather, offering me a job. A job! OMG! The catch? I graduated on Thursday, and the job started on Monday—*or there was no job.*

I was way too far along in my training to abandon ship. I had already paid for registration and travel to Chicago. Plus, my friend Susan was depending on me. Regardless of the marathon's no-refund policy, I couldn't just bail on her.

So Monday it was!

I attempted to do it all. Every day, for four straight months, I'd wake up at 5 A.M., run, take the hour-long train ride into Manhattan, work for ten-plus hours, take the hour-long train ride home, have dinner with my parents, and collapse into bed. Lather, rinse, repeat. I was absolutely exhausted and wanted to cut back on my training, but a good marathoner friend of mine said, "No way! Don't miss a day of training. Even if you run one mile and come home, it's better than nothing. If you miss even one day of training, it's too easy to miss more until you fall off the wagon." So I pushed on, running in the dark, in the rain, in ninety-degree weather with humidity that made it feel like ninety million degrees. Once I was so dehydrated that I got sick on the side of the road. I was several miles from home, without a cell phone (this was 2003!). I had no way back other than running! I was a woman on a mission.

My life centered around training and work. (Though right before I left for Chicago for the marathon, I went on the first few dates with the man I wound up marrying! But that's a whole different story.)

Marathon weekend finally arrived. My whole family supported me, standing on the sidelines wearing RUN, RANDI, RUN T-shirts. It was a fluke eighty-degree day in Chicago, definitely not ideal for running 26.2 miles. Susan and I had body-painted our arms and legs and were ready to go, hopping from foot to foot in excitement at the start line—but that's kind of my last real memory of the race. I know someone at the six-mile mark shouted, "You're almost there!" and I wanted to claw their eyes out. I remember there were just as many people holding GO CUBS! signs as GO MARATHONERS! signs, which amused me, considering it wasn't even the same sport—wait, was I playing baseball?— especially as delirium kicked in at mile 20. I hit that "wall" at mile 22, so Susan had to entice me back to reality with math. "Randi, what's two plus two? If you can answer, you can keep running!" I finally finished in four hours, twenty-nine minutes. I was congratulated with a medal, a silver metallic cape, and a beer (um? Okay!).

Regardless of a toenail loss (sign of being hard core?) and massive soreness for days, running that marathon is one of my proudest accomplishments. The most I had ever run before I started training was maybe four miles, and that's being generous. Training taught me grit and discipline, and gave me the mental strength to take on anything, no matter how hard it may be. And had it not been for my training buddy Susan, especially in those last few miles, my fitness (and life!) goals might not have become a reality. Everyone needs a coach!

Tony Horton, our Fitness Expert, is perhaps best known for his P90X exercise videos—a series that has sold a combined total of over seven million copies and has completely revolutionized the home workout. Tony trains everyone from celebrities to politicians (Speaker of the House Paul Ryan is a total Tony Horton fan boy). Aside from being one of the funniest people I've ever had the opportunity to interview on my radio show (he refers to himself as "America's Fitness Clown"), Tony is charismatic and driven. He pivoted his dream of an acting career into becoming one of the best-known fitness personalities of our time.

Tony got his start in a nontraditional way. In his free time, he began training his boss at 20th Century Fox, where he was working as a junior staffer on the movie lot in Los Angeles. Tony soon became indispensable to his employer, which led to referrals, which led to his first celebrity client, the late Tom Petty. Tony told me that Tom Petty called him up and said, "Tony, I'm going on tour. I gotta get fit. Help me!" Tony quickly made a workout regimen to get Tom into fighting shape. "I got him on the bike and had him lift heavy weights. He went off and did his tour and from then on the phone didn't stop ringing."

FITNESS PASSIONISTA

The person who always picks Fitness and has the support of their family, friends, and community.

> "I remember one day I told my mom, 'I'm not doing this anymore. It's too hard.' She said, 'Okay, no problem. Let's just give it three months and see how you feel.' Here I am, eleven years later, and I'm still going. She knew me well enough to know how disappointed I'd be if I quit, and she was right. I think about the 'what if' all the time. Surround yourself with people who want the best for you and will help you get there."
>
> **—LAURIE HERNANDEZ,**
> **GOLD MEDAL–WINNING OLYMPIC GYMNAST**

When Laurie Hernandez was only twelve years old, she took eleventh place in the junior division of the U.S. Classic. Just a few years later, she won gold in the team event for women's gymnastics in the 2016 Summer Olympics and took home the silver medal for her performance on the balance beam. It's been over a decade since Laurie first started out in gymnastics, and her eyes are still set on gold.

Laurie's accomplishments range from getting over a knee injury (which tempted her to quit) to publishing a *New York Times* bestselling book, *I Got This,* but the sacrifices she has made for her passion run much deeper. "I started homeschooling in third grade. Giving up public school, sometimes you don't mind it and other times you do. Sometimes I wish I had more friends."

Laurie also has had to sacrifice sleep, another of our precious Pick Three buckets. Sleep, which is crucial to an athlete's success, is something that Laurie struggles with. From constant travel to jet lag, the loss of sleep has almost cost her her career. "Once, I was on the balance beam. I was tired that day, but I was too scared to communicate. I just wanted to get it done and didn't want to make it a big deal—I almost felt bad saying something. I remember flipping. I threw myself off the side of the beam and fractured my wrist. It took me a few more lessons to start communicating when I'm tired, but things definitely happen for a reason."

Most people never get to experience the feeling of being in the zone, accomplishing the greatest of feats in their particular path—as Laurie has as a gold medal Olympian. She knows nothing else can give her the joy she feels when she's doing what she loves. She knows she'll have hard days, and ups and downs, but just being there, doing what she always wanted to do, is the greatest feeling ever. She advises anyone who is striving for the same sort of achievement to make sure you're doing what you love: you can't be afraid to walk away if you're on a course of action that isn't making you happy, but if you truly want to be great, then you need to go for it with every fiber in your body, and don't give yourself an out, an escape hatch.

"I almost want to say, 'Don't have a Plan B,' because if you have a backup plan, then it's like you're planning not to go all the way," Laurie told me. "Give it your all. Be hopeful."

Physically, Laurie knows life can get hard, but for her, mental adaptation is the most challenging aspect. "My brain absolutely loves to play tricks on me, so I make sure that I have moments of self-care and to remember that when I'm out there, I'm focusing on what I'm doing and not focusing on anyone else."

Laurie is a perfectionist. Even her mother tells her she's being too hard on herself, especially if she's having a rough day. Sometimes Laurie has to remind herself that there are other gymnasts out there working hard who haven't yet achieved what she's achieved. She has to switch her thought process to stay clear. She also has to remind herself how lucky she is to have a supportive family and community around her, people who encourage her and make their own sacrifices so that she can achieve excellence and truly be a Fitness Passionista.

As for where Laurie will be in the years to come, she says she's focused mainly on Work, Fitness, and Family. In the future life may shift toward Friends, but since most of her friends are gymnasts, and gymnastics is her career, her family, and her life, Fitness is an obvious dominant thing that she picks every day.

Laurie works hard at her goals. "This has taught me how to cope with being afraid and how to try new skills. I look at some of the moves they try to teach us and I'm like, 'Is that legal? That's some Star Wars stuff. I don't think it's a good idea.' When

I was younger, I would be afraid of it and not try it. But now I know I'd regret not trying. Maybe I'll fall on my butt, but I'd regret not giving it a chance."

I'm in awe of incredible athletes like Laurie and the sacrifices they have to make to achieve that level of athletic prowess. But while the rest of us might not be winning Olympic gold medals (participation trophy FTW!), we can still carve out our own fitness goals that make us feel (almost) as proud.

Even though the Chicago Marathon in 2003 was the only marathon I've run, my training taught me the importance of having daily microgoals that lead up to something bigger with a sense of accomplishment and purpose. You can't go from not running at all to running a marathon tomorrow. You have to train, build, and gradually increase mileage each week. Ever since then, I've set large fitness goals that I want to accomplish by the end of the year, something that feels really daunting but actually, when you break it down into daily chunks, is quite manageable.

Twice now I've given myself the goal of running a thousand miles in a calendar year. A thousand miles seems crazy when you look at the number as a whole, but when you break it down it's only about 2.5 miles a day, or twenty to thirty minutes of running, which I could handle—as long as I stuck with it every day. Missing a few days would mean a six-to-eight-mile run on the weekend, and that became my motivation to stick with it.

I kept a daily log so I could watch the number of miles go up, giving me a sense of accomplishment, which, in turn, fed into my professional and personal relationships. The first year I set the thousand-mile goal (2012), I ran my thousandth mile on

December 29. The next year I set that goal (2016), I completed my thousandth mile in October (!) and reset the goal to eleven hundred miles. You can do anything if you take it one day at a time.

You don't have to be a professional athlete to be a Fitness Passionista. For example, my good friend Elizabeth Weil has always prioritized exercise. She has competed in marathons, ultramarathons, Ironman races—you name it. She calls picking Fitness a "nonnegotiable" in her life, and she even met her husband while training for a triathlon. I asked her if she had ever taken time off from fitness and she said, yes, a few days while on bedrest during her first pregnancy. So anytime you are lacking the motivation to exercise, just think about Elizabeth, busy tech executive, mother of three, running dozens of miles per week—and get your butt off that sofa.

TAKE YOUR FITNESS TO THE NEXT LEVEL

Even Passionistas like to improve their game! Here are a few ideas to boost your fitness goals:

SET A MAJOR GOAL (THEN MAKE A GAME PLAN!). Everybody sets goals on January 1st. By February 1st, most people have fallen off the wagon. It's great to set big goals for yourself, but if you don't make a game plan, it's never going to happen. Break your goals down into attainable daily/ weekly action plans. Keep track of what you do, whether it's in a handwritten journal or an app in your phone (I log my workouts in the Notes app). Try to identify potential roadblocks and obstacles so you'll be prepared when they inevitably arise.

BUDDY UP. Having somebody to share your fitness journey makes it much more likely that you'll stick with it. Lots of places offer social programs or boot camps to help you ramp up your fitness goals.

DEFINE YOUR MOTIVATION. It takes a lot of discipline to stay on track and push through when things get hard. But if you're crystal clear on your motivation—*why you want to accomplish this goal*—you'll be much more likely to stay focused and disciplined.

SHOUT YOUR GOALS TO ANYONE WHO WILL LISTEN. Want to run a half marathon? Learn how to do a pull-up? Climb Kilamanjaro? If you talk about goals publicly, it makes you accountable to your network to actually do them.

YOU CAN'T OUT-TRAIN YOUR DIET. Sometimes the best thing you can do for your overall fitness is to do a complete overhaul of your diet. You can spend hours in the gym every day, but if you eat poorly, you'll never see results. Unfortunately, there's no "one size fits all" method of changing your diet. Find a program that works for you, and see how a diet makeover can ramp up your fitness goals.

FITNESS ELIMINATOR

"The best part about non-exercise is that I don't feel guilty about not going to the gym as I did several years ago when I was a 'gym-goer.' I do not miss working out one bit."

—LIZ WOLFF, FOUNDER OF CURE THRIFT SHOP

On the complete other side of the spectrum is Liz Wolff, who refers to herself as a "non-exerciser," a term she came up with in response to her extreme dislike of exercise. "I have always hated exercising and dread organized workouts. I simply don't like to work out in a conventional way and don't make it a priority in my life." Liz is not lazy nor is she unhealthy, she has a six-year-old son and owns and manages a busy retail store in New York City.

Liz simply doesn't have the time for exercise—something she knows is an all-too-common excuse. But for her, it's been at least 3 or 4 years since she's had the time to do the type of exercise that she enjoys. She won't force herself to join a gym. "I live in Manhattan so I end up walking several miles every day, but I never actually take classes or intentionally work out."

Contrary to popular belief, the decision to be a non-exerciser has not impacted her life one bit. She eats healthy food and keeps her body moving all day long at work and at home. She has no guilt about not going to the gym, and no shame about telling people she is *not* going to the gym. "I don't actively tell people that I forgo exercise, but I am definitely open about the fact that I don't work out. Other than a few physicians, no one has reacted to my lack of exercise. If anyone did react, I would think that it's pretty strange, but I would not care at all. There is much more to me than my non-exercise routine."

Liz says people who put fitness at the top of the to-do list have different priorities and ambitions. If a person wants to make exercise a top priority (or not), their personal decision is something she could care less about. "As long as you're active in other ways and eat healthy food, I think that you'll be okay. Also, I just think that there is so much more to life than being a slave to the gym. As long as you're healthy and most importantly, you FEEL great, do what works best for you."

While I'm not advocating for anyone to ever completely eliminate Fitness in their life, there are plenty of reasons why you may need to do so temporarily. If you have had periods where you have had to be a Fitness Eliminator, or maybe you're even going through one now, try to visualize an end in sight. Put a time stamp on how long this phase will last. If there's no end in sight, remind yourself of why you have had to eliminate Fitness and, if it's for a health reason outside of your control, give yourself the permission to do what you need to do right now, in order to become healthy enough again to pick Fitness in the future.

I wish I could tell you that I have come to peace over the years with my own fitness level, shape, endurance, etc.—but it's a constant struggle. I don't always eat well when I'm traveling, I gain muscle (and therefore weight) easily, and I constantly exist in the throes of a passionate love-hate relationship with my body. I remember the first time I ever spoke at a business conference, I was discussing politics and social media. When I looked at the comments online afterward, all anybody was talking about was, "Look how fat her arms are. Does she eat only Snickers bars?" It's just one of those disgusting realities that exist for women in the workplace: your appearance is up for review as much as your job performance. (Women already accomplish so much profession-ally, imagine how much more productive we'd be if we DIDN'T have to think about aesthetics so much. It's scary how much we'd dominate.) Add my love-hate body relationship onto the added fun of being pregnant twice and you've got a lifetime of therapy bills. I'd give anything to be the weight now that I was when I first thought I was "fat" in my teens.

But being healthy shouldn't just be about the number on a scale. It's about being strong, being your best self, having the energy to give your all to whatever you choose to focus on. That's why discovering my own life hack of fitness microgoals has completely changed my life. If I weren't disciplined about it, I'd probably be a Fitness Eliminator a bit more than I should. But I set goals for myself that require me to stick with it, every single day.

This past year, I set a goal for myself of forty thousand bur-pees in a calendar year. I know, I know, burpees are terrible. Literally the worst. But they're also a crazy efficient, awesome workout, and they're great for someone like me who travels so much because I don't need a fancy gym or equipment—just a small strip of hopefully prevacuumed floor. Sure, forty thousand burpees seems insane, but again, breaking it down it's only about a hundred a day (yes, *only*). That's ten to fifteen minutes of in-tense daily activity, less than the recommended average workout! When you start to think about it that way, a daily routine seems incredibly manageable. And I sure as heck didn't want to miss a day and have to do two hundred the next day! Yikes!

Fitness guru Tony Horton agrees with my idea to set yearly goals as opposed to short-term ones. "To avoid boredom, injury, and plateau, I get people to always work on weaknesses. There's nothing worse than getting bored to death and your knees are killing you. You have to open yourself up to other types of training."

Working out for fifteen minutes or jogging for twenty-five minutes on a daily basis may not sound like much to write home about, especially when you're supposed to get thirty minutes of exercise at least five times a week. But when you can say, "I ran eleven hundred miles last year," or "I did forty thousand burpees in 2017," that feels crazy awesome. A sense of pride fuels you to reach deeper in all aspects of life when you attain a new fitness level. The ability to work toward a long-term goal in small, disciplined chunks will serve you well in everything you do, personally and professionally. And dividing things up into microgoals will ensure a daily fitness regime, even if you don't have the time to pick Fitness as one of your Pick Three.

This year, my goal is to lift three million pounds of weight over the course of one calendar year. That's a whole lot of dumbbell squats and lunges. Wish me luck! I need it!

LOVING YOURSELF AND YOUR BODY

"Do I eat healthy because I love myself or do I love myself because I eat healthy?" —TIM BAUER, MOTIVATIONAL SPEAKER

In November 2010, Tim Bauer was more than two hundred pounds overweight and finally made the decision once and for all to lose weight and get his life back. He had just cheated on yet another diet and went to sleep feeling as guilty as ever. When he woke up the next day he saw a picture on Reddit of a man who had lost the same amount of weight he needed to lose, and he was inspired. He decided to go out and take a walk for the first time in years.

"I went as far as I could before I was completely out of breath, paused for a few minutes, and then walked back. When I returned, I was breathing as if I had just reached the summit of Everest. I had taken what I later counted as a 212-step walk. But here's the thing: I didn't die. And I had a good feeling that if I didn't die today, I probably wouldn't die if I did it again."

Before Tim made the decision to lose weight, he was miserable. He had given up on life, which was one of the factors that kept him morbidly obese. He had reached a low in seemingly every area of his life: his marriage was falling apart, he couldn't hold on to a job, and he felt spiritually bankrupt. Tim had grown up as a latchkey kid, and food became a source of comfort. Since both parents worked in food service, the one thing that was always at home on good days and bad days was food. Doritos became Tim's best friend, and pints of ice cream were his girlfriends in high school.

Every male over the age of thirty-five in Tim's family has had a heart attack. Tim seemed destined to go down the same path. He told me that at his heaviest, he regularly started feeling chest pains. He would later find out they were heartburn, but at the time, he was terrified. Every time he felt anything in his chest area, he immediately assumed he was having a heart attack, like all his relatives before him. Not only that, he was prediabetic, with extremely high cholesterol. Going to the doctor's office felt like going to the principal's office to get scolded for a terrible report card after ditching school all year.

It was easy to tie his disappointment in himself to his weight. He was miserable that he had lost control, which just sent him down a shame spiral in which he would make poor health decisions, which in turn only made him more miserable. It seemed like there was nothing Tim could do about it. But the day he took his walk, everything changed. In that moment, he made a first small decision to practice some self-care, to love himself, to value himself, to give himself permission to be happy. That small action turned into motivation, which turned into movement, which turned into self love.

The main motivation for the change came when Tim finally made the decision to stop settling for a life half lived. In the past, when he'd tried to lose weight, he'd get discouraged after a certain point, but this time, he was simply focusing on one pound at a time and would only brag about that pound. "I ended up losing one pound 225 times in a little over a year. I lost another twenty-five pounds in loose skin removal" (which was televised as part of TLC's *Skin Tight*).

One of the most challenging aspects of losing weight was attending social events. Tim started his journey right before the holiday season, so it meant calling ahead to homes where he would be celebrating to get permission to bring his own prepacked meal. "Everyone ended up being completely supportive, but I really couldn't bear to start cheating that early. Food felt like an addiction to me, and I didn't feel capable of moderation."

Now when Tim sees himself in the mirror, he still doesn't recognize the man he sees there. He's flabbergasted when women pay attention to him, though he doesn't feel any different as a person. His closest friends who knew him before and after tell him that he hasn't changed at all other than the exterior. "There are times I still notice myself behaving like a morbidly obese person: I break into a cold sweat when I have to walk through a crowded room, I cover my arms in pictures (something I used to do at 440 pounds to block my stomach from appearing), and I still feel an irrational fear of airplane seats."

Tim's success in weight management translated to success in work. The revenue of Tim's company increased by almost 100 percent in the year after he lost the weight. He credits this to his increased energy levels, as well as to people treating him differently. "They're more likely to listen to me in this body than my old one, and they're more likely to take me seriously (I defaulted to a clown role à la Chris Farley before). My best friend in the world tells me every day how much he loves that I'm still the same person at under two hundred pounds as I was at 440, and I am proud of that."

While Tim attributes the change to his appearance, I'm going to go out on a limb and say that it is likely the change in how he carried himself—his confidence—is what affected how others treated him. When you treat yourself like you are garbage, well, you can't be surprised when others follow suit. But when you treat yourself like you matter, like you have worth, like you're here for a bigger purpose, other people treat you that way, too.

The most important thing that anyone ever said to Tim happened two weeks into his weight-loss journey when a friend found out what he was trying to do. He helped Tim see what would happen with consistent results and explained to him that by the following Thanksgiving, if he just focused on losing two pounds every week, he could be down over a hundred pounds. "It was the first time anyone had ever looked me in the eye and said, 'I believe in you.' So the first piece of advice I would give would be to find a cheerleader."

In other words, surround yourself with supporters, rather than enablers. If your current friends aren't people who can lift you up and help you accomplish your goals, surround yourself with others who will. And those "others" can be in the form of podcasts or books, too. Tim admits, "Some of my greatest weight-loss advocates were incredible authors and speakers whom I've never met."

Tim found that both in weight loss and in professional life, we are easily overwhelmed by the size of a goal. "It's like when I tell my daughters to clean their room. They look around and they see a pile of clothes in one corner, a bunch of Pokémon cards in the other corner, and toys in another corner, and they throw up their arms and say, 'It's too much! Where do I even start?' I gently prompt them: 'Let's just start with that pair of socks. Then let's get those pants hung up, and then let's get those cards' . . . and before you know it, the room looks perfect!"

The greatest thing about Tim's metamorphosis has been the way he's been able to get close to his daughters, both figuratively and literally. Today, they can sit in his lap without his belly getting in the way. They can wrap their arms completely around him when he gives them a hug. He can take them to the park and run and play and not have to worry about his knees getting sore or his back starting to ache. "By loving myself, I taught them to do the same and learned how to truly love them."

When I asked Tim if he's happy today, he says he's as happy today as he's ever been. If you're picking up this book because you need motivation and encouragement to allow yourself to pick Fitness a bit more, Tim's advice is to take care of yourself, but don't tie your happiness and self-worth to a number on the scale. Don't fall into the trap

> of saying, "If only I could lose those fifty pounds, then I'd be happy." Be as happy with the journey as you are with the outcome, and give yourself permission to have setbacks. Tim acknowledges, "I'm not perfect and I know that I never will be, but I accept myself. I stay patient with my mistakes, and because of that, I haven't deviated from my goal weight more than five pounds, plus or minus."

Last year, to raise money for Broadway Cares, a charity that helps offset health expenses for Broadway actors suffering from illnesses such as HIV/AIDS, I somehow convinced two awesome trainers, Brian Patrick Murphy and Michael Littig, to do three hundred burpees with me on Facebook Live from Mark Fisher Fitness (best. gym. EVER. Unicorn costumes plus hard-core fitness plus Broadway show tunes—more on it shortly). We were decked out in headbands, knee socks that read BUCK FURPEES, and shirts that read NEVER MESS WITH A GIRL WHO DOES BURPEES FOR FUN. I'll admit, it was pretty brutal, and live-streamed no less, but we wound up doing 325 burpees in forty-five minutes! The fact that people were watching us live really motivated us. It also meant that I got to take the next two days off due to a very sore behind!

In high school, I was captain of the varsity fencing team. Crazy, huh? I'll admit I did it because, first, it was theatrical. Everyone sword-fights in Shakespeare plays, so it seemed like a sport that I could relate to (*en garde!*). Second, the team was just starting in my sophomore year, so everyone was brand-new at the sport; I could join without having to play catch-up to people who had been fencing for years.

TOO BUSY TO WORK OUT? TRY THESE QUICK FIXES.

Sometimes you're too busy to pick Fitness in your Pick Three. Luckily, fitness isn't a zero-sum game. Here are a few ways to Pick Fitness, even when you can't give it a lot of time:

5 MINUTES TO A GREAT WORKOUT. Whoever said you can't get a great workout in 5 minutes never tried my "50 burpees in 5 minutes" challenge. High intensity, short timeframe HIIT workouts are hugely popular. There are thousands of YouTube videos, fitness apps, and tutorials that give you a workout in a short timeframe.

DOUBLE DUTY. Have to make a call? Walk and talk. You'll be amazed how quickly a few steps here and there add up.

MORNING ROUTINE. A few yoga moves or a 60-second plank can jump-start any morning routine.

PUT YOUR MONEY WHERE YOUR HIPS ARE. Sign up for a class, book a trainer, buy new gym clothes. Make an investment you won't want to waste.

SCHEDULE IT TOMORROW. Stop beating yourself up and prioritize it tomorrow. That's the beauty of Pick Three. You can change your picks every day.

ith fencing, I had the secret advantage of being left-handed, meant I learned how to fight righties, since I practiced them all the time, but when righties came up against me petition, they had no clue what to do against their mir- e, since they also practiced against mostly righties. So I quickly rose up the ranks, winning competitions and becoming the captain of the team my senior year.

The only downside of being a leftie fencing righties who had no idea what to do against you? I got stabbed. Everywhere. I was literally covered in bruises—inside my elbows, on my neck, on my legs, to the extent that I dressed in long sleeves even in warm weather! The fencing gear covers your face and torso, but that's no match for a flailing, confused rightie with a hard metal sword. #Ouch!

But a few bruises (okay, more than a few) are nothing compared to the devastating injuries and challenges that some professional athletes need to overcome.

FITNESS RENOVATOR

The person who wants to pick Fitness but due to an unexpected life incident, has reimagined and re-envisioned the way their sport of choice would look.

> " 'Confined to a wheelchair' is a popular phrase that has always made my stomach churn. Myself and so many others in wheelchairs do not feel confined in any way but view the chair more as a tool to help us succeed."
>
> **—AARON "WHEELZ" FOTHERINGHAM,**
> **WHEELCHAIR MOTORCROSS CHAMPION**

It's amazing how many inspiring athletes there are in the world who make our own setbacks—whether they're injury or goal oriented—seem like a piece of cake. Take wheelchair motorcross champion (WCMX), Aaron "Wheelz" Fotheringham, who was born with Spina Bifida, a defect of the spinal cord which resulted in nonuse of his legs. Aaron was determined to make it work.

Aaron was aware from an early age that he was a bit different, but it wasn't a bad thing. He felt he had advantages that his friends didn't. When his friends would ride their bikes around the neighborhood, he would ditch his crutches and take his wheelchair so he could keep up. "I just always did my best to do whatever the other kids were doing."

Aaron remembers the first time he went to the skatepark with his brother and father. Usually he'd just sit and watch from behind a fence. But his family urged him to try the ramps on his wheelchair. "[It] was pretty rough! The first couple times dropping into the quarter pipe I faceplanted and jammed my wrists. I think the reason I tried again after crashing was because I realized that it wasn't as bad as I had imagined it to be, and I think from there my adrenaline took over and I just really wanted to land it!"

And land it he did! Aaron has since gone on to win various WCMX competitions, even taking home the gold at a few freestyle BMX competitions. He's progressed in his wheelchair trickery so much that he's even landed a *double backflip* in his wheelchair, which led him to perform with the death-defying sports collective, Nitro Circus. But one major accomplishment Aaron is proud of (besides jumping a full size Mega Ramp and landing a 50-foot gap in his chair (OMG)!) is helping others, especially young kids, see their chair as something to have fun with rather than a limiting medical device. "It truly is all in the way you view your chair or 'restriction.' I always say, 'I don't suffer from Spina Bifida, it suffers from ME!'"

Aaron got his nickname WHEELZ in middle school because he was always zooming around the halls superfast and jumping the stairs. Kids started calling him "Wheels," and he changed the S to a Z. "The biggest misconception about being in a wheelchair is that people view it as a prison," says Aaron. "Don't let fear rule your imagination. It's always scary at the top of the ramp, but you just have to visualize yourself succeeding and stay positive—and I feel that applies to every big/scary goal!" Which is solid advice for any industry, career, or lifestyle choice, Mega Ramp or not.

Although he's won numerous accolades, Aaron's wheeling skills have not yet reached the level at which he wants to be. Currently he's working on landing a bunch of new tricks, like a double front flip (whoa). And as for the WCMX, Aaron is helping its growth potential by inspiring and encouraging people all over the world into having fun with their wheelchairs in skateparks. Wear helmets and pads, please! (Yes, I am a mother to two boys—obvi.)

Fear is oftentimes our worst enemy when it comes to trying anything new. Whether it's opening your own business, going in for an interview, sending out résumés, or doing a double back flip in a wheelchair, our fear can be the single thing that holds us back from trying. Or, it's what leads to our failure because we hesitate so much in those final moments before making a decision that we fall flat on our face.

I remember how scared I was to start my own business. I was worried I was making a huge mistake. Fear told me that I wasn't good enough, smart enough, fill-in-the-blank enough to go out on my own. Fear had crippled me in a way that made me second guess my talents and hurt my first few major decisions as my own boss. But, like Aaron, once I realized all my failures weren't anywhere near as bad as my fear told me they would be, I dusted myself off and went for a double backflip of my own.

Now that I subscribe to the Pick Three theory of getting s%@t done, fear hasn't played as large of a role in my life—in fact, fear isn't even a supporting character. It's more like the extra that may be part of the B-roll footage. When you can only Pick Three, there's no open slot to waste by Picking Fear. Like Aaron said, when you visualize yourself succeeding and stay positive, you can accomplish your goals, no matter what they are.

Yet sometimes our goals aren't to jump a 50-foot gap in a wheelchair, or finish a marathon, or even wake up in the morning to get a short jog in. Sometimes they're not even about us at all. Sometimes, we wind up picking Fitness to support a loved one's Pick Three.

FITNESS SUPERHERO

This person becomes lopsided toward Fitness in support of a loved one.

"I know that there's a limited window of opportunity for Scott as he gets older, so we need to focus on his career right now. When he's done racing and being competitive, then we can put more emphasis on my career."

—JENNY JUREK, COACH AND WIFE TO ULTRAMARATHONER, SCOTT JUREK

Jenny Jurek is the founder and lead designer of Rain or Shine Design, an outdoor-clothing-apparel brand. She's also the crew chief and coach of her husband's professional ultrarunning career.

Scott Jurek broke the Appalachian Trail speed record in 2015—covering the 2168.1-mile route in forty-six days, eight hours, and seven minutes—with the support of his wife. Jenny met Scott during her own running journey. They met when she first started running in Seattle. They were friends and in the same running group for about eight years before they started dating. "By the time we got together in 2008, I was an avid runner and had run many ultramarathons, including a one-hundred-mile race."

When Scott is racing or doing a long multiday adventure such as the Appalachian Trail, Jenny's job is to meet him at multiple places a day and be a roving support crew. When they meet up, she refills his water bottles, resupplies his sport energy foods, changes out his gear, offers him real food, makes smoothies—you name it. After he gets back on the trail, she gets gas and groceries, and navigates her way to the next meeting spot. At night, she makes dinner, checks him for ticks, goes over the maps, and plans out their next day's stops. "We are a team, and he supports me so much in our daily lives that I'm happy to support his goals. It's definitely a two-way street. When he's not racing, he's always helping me pursue my dreams. We share a lot of the same passions, so it's always a fun adventure crewing for him."

Of course, Jenny has goals of her own, too. She was an avid rock climber way before she started running. She still has big climbing aspirations and running goals—those never go away. Scott always supports her dreams, and they've gone on some great climbing adventures together.

Because Jenny still has her career as an apparel designer (besides her own company, she works as a freelance designer of athletic apparel and soft goods for outdoor companies including Patagonia, Salomon, and Brooks), she's able to combine her lifestyle with her work and can do so while helping Scott. "It's really just a matter of juggling our schedules. I feel like I can maintain my own identity while crewing for Scott. He is very respectful of my personal growth, and we make time for both of us."

But even for normal, everyday people, who aren't running hundreds of miles or breaking Guinness records, fitness can be an incredible way to bond with and support a loved one. Maybe you're cheering on a family member participating in a 5K fun run. Maybe you're watching your six-year-old son level up to a new belt color in tae kwon do (which I proudly did recently!). Maybe you're supporting a friend at a varsity or college-level sporting event, or setting a precedent for fitness in a new romantic relationship, which will be something important in your Pick Three for life.

Bonus points if you can also participate! You know I always love when you can crank out two of your Pick Three goals at the same time! Whether it's going for a walk or run, or taking a lesson in a sport like golf, skiing, or tennis, engaging in fitness with a loved one is a great way to get healthy and create memories. Engaging in fitness activities with a partner enables you to pick Fitness AND pick Family at the same time.

When I pick Fitness, when I prioritize my own health, when I feel good about my body and my fitness accomplishments, I do better in EVERYTHING. I'm a better mom, a better partner, a better boss, and a better friend. I carry myself taller professionally. But, as with most anything in life, when it comes to fitness you have to know yourself. For me, I know that setting big goals and dividing them into microgoals sets me up for maximum success. I also know bringing in other people helps keep me accountable, forcing me to prioritize fitness, even when everything else in my life is screeching to put it on the back burner.

The good news is that even if you don't have people in your life who can keep you accountable, technology can provide that support. There are many helpful, fun, and even silly wearable health trackers, fitness apps, and devices that help keep us motivated, track our progress, and keep us on task. I have found personally that wearing a Fitbit is really helpful in providing that extra boost of motivation to get out walking. Once, I was at nine thousand steps and needed to go out to an event, and my son offered to put my Fitbit on his wrist and walk in circles around our apartment until it got to ten thousand—all for the steep, steep price of one dollar. Not exactly the point of a health tracker, but it was pretty adorable. And hey, there might be an actual business somewhere in there about helping other people reach their fitness goals! Luckily, living in New York City and not owning a car is pretty much like having a pedometer built into your lifestyle.

Aside from my Fitbit holding me accountable, I'm lucky enough to be under the tutelage of an incredible trainer at one of my favorite fitness obsessions, Mark Fisher Fitness.

FITNESS MONETIZER

Someone whose current career and mission is around creating products for Fitness!

"We believe in, have built, and continually work on creating COMMUNITY."

—BRIAN PATRICK MURPHY,
TRAINER AT MARK FISHER FITNESS

If you remember my burpees goal from earlier, you'd also remember the amazing gym where my burpees training first got started. There are lots of Fitness Monetizers out there—gyms, personal trainers, classes, fitness apparel, etc.—but I have to say that Mark Fisher Fitness is one of the most fun and unique places I have ever seen in this industry. From costumes to confetti and glitter to showtime playlists, all while seeing people accomplish serious fitness goals, MFF (aka the Enchanted Ninja Clubhouse of Glory and Dreams) has become an integral part of my life, and many other New Yorkers' lives as well.

I have been training with Brian Patrick Murphy, trainer, sales manager, and self-proclaimed minister of belief at Mark Fisher Fitness, for over a year now. Brian and I crush some serious weight together and do more burpees than should be legal, but we also laugh a lot and have tons of fun. I asked Brian if he could help define what makes MFF so special, both as a place to train and as a place to work, and how that has contributed to their success.

Brian told me that what makes MFF so impossible NOT to show up for is its community. "'Community' is definitely becoming more of a buzzword and trend in the fitness industry. We were really at the front of this movement."

Community is something not many gyms can tout. Think of the last time you showed up to work out. How many people did you say hello to? How many people knew your name? At Mark Fisher Fitness, everyone knows everyone else and cheers them on (sometimes even dumping glitter on them), so motivation comes from a place of togetherness. In fact, every workout begins with a question that everyone in the room answers, which immediately fosters a sense of personal connection, friendship, and team spirit.

Brian truly embodies the MFF tagline: "Ridiculous Humans, Serious Fitness." He can often be found in the gym wearing hot pink from head to toe, while motivating people to accomplish fitness goals beyond what they ever dreamed possible. He says that teamwork and results can't be achieved without the un-mentioned third ingredient: infinite heart. "I believe that's what really makes our community special. We aren't perfect, but we have infinite heart and our ninjas really feel it and believe it."

What's a ninja, you ask? Some gyms call their clients cus-tomers, some call them users. MFF calls them ninjas, which just furthers the sense of fun and community. Brian let me in on a little secret: the ninjas have become MFF's best marketing strat-egy. "The amazing experiences and the way people feel by being part of this community is by far our most effective marketing strategy—something that gets spread by word of mouth."

DON'T FORGET THESE AREAS OF FITNESS!

I know I'm spending a lot of time talking about physical fitness, but fitness is a catch-all bucket for health and well-being. Make sure you don't forget about these important areas for being fit:

SPIRITUALITY. Feeling connected to something bigger than yourself is key to a sense of health and well-being.

MINDFULNESS. Many successful business executives have a daily meditation, mindfulness, or deep breathing practice. Having an outlet for stress management is beneficial in more ways than you could dream possible.

NUTRITION. Remember that your body is your only true home. You can't achieve peak health and happiness without nourishing it properly.

SHARPNESS. Keep your brain sharp and mentally stimulated. If you're in a job that is repetitive, or you've reached an age where you can feel yourself becoming a bit more forgetful or absent-minded, seek out activities, apps, and games for staying mentally sharp.

GRATITUDE. Write a "thank you" note, go around the dinner table to say what you're grateful for, or spend 30 seconds feeling thankful. It pays off in spades. (I'm thankful to you for reading my book!)

AT MARK FISHER FITNESS, SUCCESS IS DEFINED BY THE PEOPLE YOU surround yourself with, and since they have amazing people on the staff and as ninjas, transforming lives through fitness becomes addicting. "My favorite part of my job is watching people transform their lives. I have the good fortune of selling memberships AND training ninjas on a daily basis. I get to watch understandably terrified people come and transform their lives. From day one throughout their journey, I feel honored to be a part of every step along the way. I get cards, e-mails, posts every day from ninjas thanking me for changing, and even SAVING, their lives." Come on now, how many gyms can say they do that for their members?

Though Mark Fisher Fitness encourages costumes, capes, unicorn horns, loud music, rainbows, glitter paint, and neon, Brian says the biggest misconception of the gym is that they are *too* silly. "We have an unbelievably serious fitness approach and a dedication to the most cutting-edge exercise and nutrition out there. Our fitness team is remarkable. We get next-level results."

I was curious, since fitness is an area that combines both inner health and outer physical appearance, do successful Fitness Monetizers feel any pressure to be in great shape and look amazing all the time? I asked Brian if he feels like he has to pick Fitness every day in his own life because, not only is it his job, but because we all have off days. He said that the pressure he feels is mostly from himself. "My biggest value is to be a leader. I believe that a great first step of leadership is to lead by example. So no matter what I look like or exactly how much I can lift or fast I can run, my leadership comes from showing up consistently over and over and over again for many weeks, months and years."

Brian also said to others "great shape" means different things. "I'm sure that to many fitpros, I'm not in insanely great shape. But, to many people in the general population, I might look to be in what they could perceive as "unattainable shape."

The real answer for Brian is both yes and no. "If I left the fitness industry tomorrow I would hold myself accountable to the same things I do now." Brian doesn't feel the need to compete with the young up-and-coming fitpros of tomorrow. He doesn't worry that his colleagues are stronger or more shredded than he could ever dream of being. His pressure and accountability is held only to himself to be the BEST version of Brian that he possibly can. "How you do anything is how you do everything. I want to hold myself to a higher standard in all realms."

As Tony Horton says, "Your purpose is to do better things in life and feel better into your thirties, forties, fifties, and beyond."

WHEN PICKING FITNESS IS MORE THAN GOING TO THE GYM

Claudia Christian may be best known for her role as Commander Susan Ivanova in the science fiction television series *Babylon 5,* but her main work is talking about alcoholism and how to treat it. As she revealed in her book *Babylon Confidential*, Claudia struggled from about age thirty-seven to age forty-four with an alcohol use disorder and felt the pressure of maintaining her looks so that she could continue in her chosen profession: acting. "I actually prayed for work because I was disciplined enough to not drink at work or before work, so I figured if I got a job I could remain sober. Unfortunately, addiction throws your energy off and makes you insecure and depressed, so the jobs weren't exactly pouring in. I kept myself busy flipping homes, which was a wonderful creative outlet and physical activity, but the wine did put on some extra pounds."

One of the most humiliating times of Claudia's life was when her manager told her to lose weight, which had never happened to her in her acting career. "I took up boxing and Pilates and did tons of cardio but would sometimes have a drink before doing these activities. It was awful carrying around this charade of being healthy when I was clearly not."

Fitness was always a priority in Claudia's life. She'd do an hour of cardio five or six times a week as well as lifting weights, doing yoga and sit-ups, and so on. "My father is eighty-four years old and still plays tennis every morning. He walks his dog miles and miles every day, and my mother does Pilates and swims. They are both excellent role models and proof that staying active positively affects your life on many levels. Staying active has always been important to me. I believe it helps the body maintain a healthy endorphin level and relieves stress, anxiety, and a host of other maladies."

Claudia was a binge drinker, so the majority of her time would be spent being fit and healthy and on track, then, about every four to six months, she would "disappear" into wine. "My relapses became worse and it took longer to recover from them. I feel peace now and I have forgiven myself, but at the time I felt enormous guilt for what I put my body through, and I thank God every day that I am healthy and strong despite having had a devastating illness."

Claudia was happy to "come out" as an addict back in 2010. She had enormous support from her fans, which made her feel loved and accepted. "Genre fans (science fiction and fantasy) are truly remarkable people. They embrace each other and support each other in their common love of these genre TV shows and films, and they love and accept the actor who played their favorite character. I played a very heroic character in *Babylon 5,* so I was extremely reluctant to admit fallibility, but when I finally did it was liberating, to say the least.

"The more we share our own personal burdens, the easier it is for others to do the same. Shame and stigma should not exist. Alcohol use disorders are brain disorders. No one picks up a glass of wine with the hopes of becoming enslaved to it. Because it is a progressive condition, it sneaks up on you over years, decades even. I drank safely and moderately for twenty years before I noticed anything amiss, so it's not exactly something you can plan for.

"I would say to people who know an addict to be loving and compassionate. Judging someone for something they cannot control is akin to judging someone with cancer or a birth defect or a mental illness. Think before you speak, and if you have nothing helpful or loving to say then don't say anything. Words can be incredibly hurtful, and words such as 'weak,' 'lazy,' 'immoral,' 'a drunk,' 'in the bag,' 'loaded,' etc. can horribly damage to someone who is already in the deepest pit of hell. I have forgiven people who have said unkind things to me or about me, and I do not engage in social media because so much of it is hateful. You have people ironically hiding behind faith-based or upbeat monikers and then spitting out hateful diatribes against me simply because I chose a scientifically proven way to treat my addiction as opposed to a 'traditional' method. There are men rambling about my looks after viewing my TEDx talk, as if that has anything to do with my message. It is a waste of time to read these things. One must carry on with belief and faith and ignore the trolls and haters. They come from a place of misinformation and a clear lack of desire to learn. Hate is everywhere—but so, thankfully, is love."

THESE BOOTS ARE MADE FOR WALKING

Fitness is more than putting on sneakers, hitting the gym, running an ultramarathon, or winning a gold medal. It encompasses all aspects of health—mental, physical, and emotional. When we talk about picking Fitness, I am referring to all areas of your health and well-being. Some areas of health include sweating, but many do not.

If you feel like you're doing a great job at prioritizing fitness, make sure you're considering all the areas of fitness and ask yourself if you're missing anything. Maybe you're a rock star at going to the gym every day, but you're deeply unhappy emotionally. Or maybe you're in a place where you're happy with yourself, but need to remind yourself to be more mindful and present in your life.

And if you'd like to pick Fitness a bit more? Welcome to the club. No, seriously, it's easy to prioritize work and all the other people in our lives and to forget about prioritizing ourselves. So the first step is to forgive yourself. Then get out a journal, write down some goals, call a friend, and make yourself accountable for investing in yourself and making self-care a priority. If you currently pick Fitness once a week, set a goal to pick it three times, whether by Fitness you mean heading to a gym, heading to a shrink, or heading to a corner of the room for your meditation practice.

You deserve a better, healthier, cleaner life. We only get one go-around on this planet. So whether you're feeling run-down, unhealthy, injured, or unmotivated, always know the power to change comes from within.

Friends

"If someone feels lonely and has no one to share their disappointments and successes, it might suggest that they should spend more time nurturing friendships."

—IRENE S. LEVINE. PH.D.. FRIENDSHIP EXPERT

I'm going to be really honest with you—this chapter was by far the most difficult for me. Even though I have a lot of "friends" by social media standards, I have far fewer people in my life who I am truly close to and spend a lot of time with. Part of this is because I love spending time with my family. I have a spouse who I consider my best friend on earth. And I love the people I work with (after all, I chose to either hire or partner with all of them!). But a big part of it is also that there's just not enough time in the day to choose everything, and when push comes to shove, I just don't find myself choosing to be lopsided in the Friends category. Maybe that will change when I'm older and no longer have young kids at home, or maybe when I take a few paces back from working so hard (ha ha, good joke). I see people with rich social lives and think, #squadgoals, but then I quickly go back to my regularly scheduled life where I continue to prioritize friends at the very bottom.

Another reason I don't prioritize Friends very often is—I'll let you in on a huge secret—I'm actually a total introvert. If you've met me in person, or seen me sing in public, or heard me deliver a speech while cracking jokes, you'd probably never believe it, but it's all just a persona I've learned to cultivate for professional reasons. After speaking in public, all I want to do is be alone for several hours and stare at a wall. I enjoy being around people, but it also drains me, which is why after a long day of work, where most of my time is spent being a professional extrovert, the very last thing I want—or need—is to be surrounded by even more people.

Meeting new people is especially difficult for an introvert. Which meant that when my husband started at Stanford Business School while I was working at Facebook, I had to take a deep breath and prepare to meet hundreds of new people who would become an important part of my husband's life for the next two years.

The spouses of business school students are called SOs (for "significant others"), and as Brent's SO, I was invited to attend many events. Since I was working 24/7 at a start-up, it was hard for me to attend most things, but I made a pretty good effort, considering.

These events were fascinating studies of human behavior, especially for SOs like myself. In the first weeks of business school, at the earliest of these events, classmates were meeting one another, networking up a storm. At first someone would shake my hand, offering their greetings and salutations, but as soon as they heard I was just an SO, that greeting quickly turned to *sayonara* as off the business student went to find someone who better mattered in terms of their career.

It was frustrating, difficult, and humbling all at the same time. I wanted to spend time with my husband and his classmates, but I felt like I was already maxed out in terms of the number of friends I had time for, so I had absolutely no use for people who didn't give me the time of day. I could quickly tell the cats from the canaries by who wanted to be our BFFs only after realizing I worked for Facebook.

Luckily, there were a few wonderful people in his class who treated SOs differently. They didn't judge people by how useful they were to their career, and some of those people are among my best friends now. One in particular, Rebecca Schapiro, is still my go-to travel buddy when I get invited to speak around the world. She's joined me on trips to places like Kuwait, Denmark, and Argentina. I count my SO blessings every day to have a trustworthy, long-lasting friend like her.

Come to think of it, I'm actually glad to have had that litmus test, too, because the friends that emerged from those business school years are some of the best, most solid people in our lives.

FRIENDS PASSIONISTA

This person is excellent at prioritizing Friends in their Pick Three; it comes easily and naturally.

> *"Our connections make the world a more vibrant and interesting place. It drives innovation and curiosity and social good. Without connections, we'd all be completely isolated."*
> —SUSAN MCPHERSON,
> FOUNDER OF MCPHERSON STRATEGIES

Some friends are fabulous connectors. They manage to stay in touch with everyone they meet and have close groups of friends that stand the test of time, no matter what. I wanted to understand what goes on in the mind of someone who prioritizes their friends so much that they earn the title of being "the ultimate connector." So I decided to speak with Susan McPherson, our Friends Passionista.

McPherson Strategies, the company Susan founded, is a consultancy focused on the intersection between brands and social good. She's been making connections for people since she was ten years old, and told me about memories of doing so at summer camp, in her Brownie and Girl Scout troops, and on her gymnastics team in college. Some people are just born social.

A lover of people, extraordinarily curious about what motivates them, drives them forward, and interests them, Susan has always been fascinated by meeting people and getting to know them. She believes that to make lasting connections you must have a solid memory, be intellectually curious, be positive and outgoing. And making connections between other people feels like a dopamine shot to her soul. She gets joy when her connections lead to a positive outcome.

The biggest challenge to Susan is when connections die on the vine and don't lead to anything (even, at minimum, a friendship). "We live in a world where having friends from all over with different interests, cultural heritages, backgrounds, and goals makes for a richer world." Thankfully, Susan cannot recall a connection that let her down, but there have been a few times when she has made major introductions and then never received a thank you or even an acknowledgment. "The first time that happened, it hurt, but over time, I realized that I don't do the connecting to be recognized. I do it to make sh*t happen!"

Her advice for other professional connectors is to do it not to get ahead but to learn from others, as each person you meet will be a conduit to their unique experiences. "Be open and warm and truly follow up with a meaningful note. Your world will be richer for doing so. And then go so far as to introduce the new contacts to others in your world."

What Susan winds up sacrificing, in order to be a connector, is her time. But she says time comes back to her in spades, as each connection she makes opens up a new opportunity that can lead to all sorts of good. There are times where she does feel overwhelmed and wonders why she spends so much time putting two and two together. But then a note from someone she put in touch with someone else will come through and re-remind her why making connections is ALWAYS worth the effort.

Out of the literally *hundreds* of connections Susan has made, one particularly sticks with her most—she was able to leverage her social circle to secure a one-hundred-thousand-dollar grant for a dear friend who was starting a pilot program in Pittsburgh called Hello Neighbor, which helps connect Syrian refugees with local buddy families. Susan believed strongly in the cause, and in her friend Sloane, who was starting the program, and it made Susan proud and thrilled to be able to leverage her social relationships to help Sloane get a program with so much good karma off the ground.

Susan believes our connections make the world a more vibrant and interesting place. Connections drive innovation and curiosity and social good. Without connections, we'd all be completely isolated.

If you can relate to Susan and people refer to you as a connector, my hat goes off to you. Just make sure that you can separate out the true friends from people who simply want something, so you don't end up giving up a lot of time to "users." For those who are less comfortable than Susan with being so social and maintaining lots of relationships, she recommends building in lightweight connections to your daily schedule. "Maintaining connections is not as challenging and time consuming as one might think. Truly, it means occasional outreach BEFORE you need something, outreach simply for the sake of saying 'Hello, how are you? I value having you in my life.'"

As you get older, it gets harder and harder to meet new friends. I was recently talking about this over dinner with another couple we're friendly with, and we realized that when you're younger and it's just you, it's really easy to make and prioritize friendships. But as we age, marry, and start families, there's suddenly a slew of criteria a potential friend needs to meet in order to make it into the inner circle. You have to:

- Like the person
- Like their SO
- Like the way they and their SO treat one another
- Like their children
- Make sure your children like their children
- Like the way they parent their children
- Like the fact that they don't have children or an SO

#OH #MY

Looking at friendships this way is completely exhausting and unrealistic, which is why, sadly, having a social life is the first thing to get deprioritized, especially when you have young children at home and/or a busy career. Sometimes it's easier to make friends through your SO. And sometimes, as in the case of business school mixers, it's not.

These experiences got me thinking about people who, whether by choice or by necessity, don't have access to their friends any longer. What happens if being lopsided means you literally *cannot* be in contact with your friends? I started thinking about astronauts who are away in space for months at a time. I thought about the countless Uber drivers I've spoken with, who talk about moving to the United States to work and send money back home, even though it means not seeing their spouses or children for years at a time. I thought about people who have "toxic" friend groups that they finally find the courage to break free from. And I thought about people who need to suddenly change their identity and cut off ties with the name, the life they've always known, in order to escape a dangerous situation.

HOW TO BE A BETTER FRIEND (AND WHAT TO DO IF YOU'VE MESSED UP)

When you're busy with work, family, and other areas of your life, it's easy to let your friendships fall to the wayside. If you find yourself in a place where you would like to Pick Friends a bit more, or if you've screwed up and can't figure out how to redeem yourself, here are a few thoughts on how to clean up the mess:

LISTEN/NO JUDGMENT. Try listening more than speaking. Make sure any advice you give comes from a place of zero judgment. It's definitely an exercise in restraint, but the payoff will be huge.

BE GOOD TO YOUR WORD. We've all had a situation where we promised to do something and then couldn't live up to our promise. It feels awful. It's far better to say no up front rather than to try and be a people pleaser.

SHOW UP. Plain and simple, be there. Don't be a fair-weather friend. Be present when your friends need you. Even when you're not thrilled about a position your friend is in, you can still support them.

BE TRULY HAPPY FOR YOUR FRIENDS. Even if you're jealous, green with envy, wishing with every fiber of your being that it was happening for you instead of for them, *don't make it about you*. Be happy for your friends and it will come back around in time.

APOLOGIZE! And mean it. Don't make excuses. Don't try to pin the blame on someone or something else. Admit when you messed up and move on. We all make mistakes. The way we handle those mistakes shows what we're really made of.

FRIENDS ELIMINATOR

This person chooses NOT to prioritize Friends in their Pick Three, repeatedly.

> *"When you're alone and have no support network this can really become a challenge. You need a trusted friend or responsible family member to facilitate the shipping of a credit card or payment of bills."*

> **—KIMBERLEY BULKLEY, MONITORING OFFICER AT OSCE SPECIAL MONITORING MISSION UKRAINE**

Kimberley Bulkley tells me it's difficult to give her profession a title. "If I have to tick a box, I usually choose 'International Development,' but this really is not accurate." Kimberley was a Russian language/international relations major who graduated in 1991 during the heady days of perestroika and glasnost—when the collapse of the Soviet Union led to renewed relations between the United States and the Russian Federation. Fittingly, Mikhail Gorbachev even spoke at her graduation in 1992.

Kimberley first went to Moscow in 1991, arriving three days after members of the Soviet Union's government attempted a coup d'état to take control of the country from Gorbachev. In 1996 Kimberley returned to the States to attend law school, but soon found herself back in the former Soviet Union. She joined the Organization for Security and Cooperation in Europe (OSCE) and moved to Vienna, Austria, where the organization has its headquarters. She worked with field missions to support government efforts to combat corruption and money laundering.

She first took a post as the OSCE's economic and environmental adviser in Tashkent, Uzbekistan, and a year and a half later transferred to Bishkek, Kyrgyzstan, where she spent four years in the same position. Later she was sent to Kabul for what she was told would be a five-year assignment. She was there for only a year.

From Asia to the Ukraine, Kimberley has not been in the same place longer than a few years. Her chosen profession is a challenging one, not only for the way it helps maintain peaceful conflict in the world, but also in how she manages her personal business from outside the States. "For example, your credit card is compromised and the company wants to send you a new one, but they can't ship the card to a war zone, but you need a credit card to book air tickets for your next vacation." Kimberley has definitely taken the road less traveled, and by doing so, she is our Friends Eliminator.

For years Kimberley made a lot of effort to keep in touch with friends in the U.S. "I sent cards, wrote e-mails, commented on Facebook, tried to organize regular Skype conversations, always forewarned when I was coming to visit, brought them presents, and dedicated time for them even when exhausted from travel. When I stopped making all these efforts, most of these friendships dissipated into thin air. I understood that although we had been friends, they simply were too busy with their own lives or couldn't relate to me anymore. I don't know if this is a uniquely U.S. phenomenon, but I do believe our lifestyle places less value on substantive deep friendships. Or perhaps it is just an issue of if they can't physically see you then you simply cease to exist in their reality."

Kimberley told me that when you work overseas most of the friendships you form are with people who are living the same lifestyle. You end up with a place to stay in almost every country in the world, but seldom have close friendships.

Technology has made all the difference for Kimberley's maintaining long-distance communication. "I exchange short notes with family and friends on Facebook Messenger, on Skype, or by e-mail on virtually a daily basis. Sometimes we are able to coordinate meet-ups in airport lounges when our travel schedules mesh. Sometimes they are attending a conference in the same country where I'm working. Sometimes we organize a reunion during a vacation somewhere. Everything depends on everyone's flexibility and desire to actually maintain the friendship."

As of now, the most important relationship for Kimberley is

the one she maintains with her parents. "They're in their mid-eighties, and visiting them is my priority. Since their time on the planet is limited, most vacations are spent helping and spending time with them."

Whether you're a Friends Eliminator or not, there is one situation many of us have in common, in which you basically have to start from scratch, meet all new people, reinvent yourself, and make friends anew—and that's going to college.

FRIENDS RENOVATOR

Someone who has to rethink and rebuild their Friends circle.

> *"Just like in any other stage of your life, friendships in college are important because they (ideally) provide a crucial system of mutual empathy and support."*
>
> **—JULIE ZEILINGER, FOUNDER AND EDITOR OF WOMEN'S MEDIA CENTER'S FBOMB BLOG**

Julie Zeilinger's *FBomb* is a feminist blog and community for teens and young adults. Julie's book *College 101: A Girl's Guide to Freshman Year* was written after she graduated college in 2015. *College 101* is a guide to everything college, including making friends. Julie is our Friends Superhero.

"Making new friends isn't difficult for *every* freshman," says Julie. "There are freshmen who make meaningful connections with others quickly and easily. But there are also plenty of people who struggle to make friends for a variety of reasons."

Julie cites students who are homesick, for example, as those who might struggle to be social while they're acclimating to their new home on campus. "Moving to a new town, a different state, or even a completely unique subculture of the country can be a huge emotional and cultural adjustment for many students. If you're from New York City, it might take a while to adjust to the culture of a largely conservative, southern campus—and it might be difficult to forge friendships with people who don't share this initial discomfort." Julie recommends looking at embedding yourself in a new, challenging environment with people different from you as a great opportunity to grow.

There are challenges for shy or introverted students to motivate themselves to be outgoing enough to meet new people, as well. Julie says that for those who value meaningful connections, it doesn't help that the majority of conversations they have during orientations are inevitably superficial. For those used to the kind of easy interactions that come from years of being around the same group of friends—people who already understand and accept your quirks—it can be challenging and even exhausting to try to make new friends.

In high school, Julie had five best friends who essentially were her entire social world. "We did everything together and knew the intimate details of each other's lives. We all ended up at different colleges, though. Although I will always be thankful for those incredibly real connections, I think that benchmark for friendship made it all the more difficult for me to feel like I was successfully connecting with new people during the first few weeks of school."

At college, Julie had a roommate and a few others she could semi-rely on in her freshman year, but what she found most difficult was wading through the annoying (yet necessary) shallow conversations that constantly followed the same pattern: name, hometown, expected major, reason for choosing this school, etc.

The same is true for postcollege life, too. We get sucked up into our own worlds around our jobs and our families, so we forget to forge new relationships. Julie reminded me that she can't develop new friendships "without constantly putting myself out there (despite my naturally introverted nature), and by pushing myself way past my comfort zone. I joined extracurricular groups and a sorority, and made a point to talk to students in my classes and around campus."

In terms of advice on how to do it, Julie says there's a popular theory that college is *the* opportunity to invent a new persona for ourselves, "that we can be whoever we have always wanted to be, but may have been discouraged from being while growing up. Those who subscribe to that theory also tend to find friends who they believe would fit that persona."

But perhaps being somebody else isn't the best way to begin a new, hopefully lasting friendship. Julie argues that the college experience isn't an opportunity to create a new persona, but rather an opportunity to get to know who we've *always* been but have been encouraged to repress. "The process of becoming acquainted with that true self is undeniably informed by the people we surround ourselves with."

It's so easy to relegate yourself to hanging out with the same type of people you did in high school: if you're a theater person, it's easy to gravitate toward other people in the drama program; if you're an environmentalist, there are undoubtedly countless eco-enthusiasts ready to reach out to you. But college campuses are full of passionate, diverse students with unique talents and interests. Julie recommends making it your personal mission to find somebody radically different from yourself and befriend them. "Although it's great to find people who understand you on an intimate level, who can relate to you in a specific way, it's also vitally important to meet people who maintain different perspectives and values than you do. Maybe the friendship will work in the long term and maybe it won't, but it will definitely be a valuable experience in some way."

High school friendships will change once you go off to college, as college friendships may change once you graduate, an inevitable consequence of time and distance. "You're likely embedded in different cultures, surrounded by different people and other influential factors, and will all personally change in ways that create an unprecedented gap."

But while your experiences at college may differ, you can preserve your bond by substantively sharing those experiences with your old high school friends. "College students are all constantly busy, but if you want to maintain a friendship, it's essential to keep in touch in a way that may be facilitated but not defined or restricted by technology. When you connect with old friends, actually fill them in on your life—even if you're dealing with complicated feelings or detailed situations specific to your group of college friends."

To keep friendships from becoming superficial, Julie says you can't relegate your conversations to superficial topics. "Really keep your friends up to date when you talk. So many times during my freshman year, I would catch up with my high school friends and realize I had somehow just *not* told them about something pretty significant that had happened in my life. It made them feel like I had purposely kept something important from them, which probably made them doubt our bond."

And always remember to cut your friends some slack (especially if you're subscribing to the Pick Three theory, which may have your BFFs picking everything *but* Friends). "You're all going to change in college, and none of you can take that change personally. Try not to judge your friends for any actions that seem out of character, but rather try to understand that they're dealing with new situations and new people and are trying to find their place in it all. If you're in a friendship for the long haul, you need to be willing to make it through some bumps in the road and be supportive and understanding even when it might be challenging to do so."

To Julie, friendships aren't just important in the context of the immediate college experience, either; they can be influential beyond it. "Having a strong network of friends can be incredibly beneficial to women's professional lives—whether your friends end up working in the same industry with you or not. Entering the workforce presents a whole new array of challenges and experiences, and having the support of people you know and can trust is a crucial tool to thriving in that new stage of your life."

People who are having a hard time making friends should take a step back and consider who they have been trying to befriend, Julie says. "It's often valuable to put ourselves in new environments and situations and challenge ourselves to break out of our comfort zones. Doing so can not only teach us about ourselves, but expose us to new things—and, of course, new people."

And as for those of us who are awkward, which is probably an overwhelming majority of us, rather than viewing our awkward behavior as something that detracts from our appeal, Julie says we should understand that many see it as a sign of our honesty and authenticity. "Anyone who can't accept a little bit of awkwardness may not prove to be the most empathetic or caring friend, anyway, so embracing our awkwardness may actually prove a good litmus test for how we connect with others."

We've all had situations where we've had to start from scratch. Whether starting a new school, moving to a new city, or starting a new job, it's always difficult to start from scratch, building relationships and trust. At the same time, it's also quite exciting, getting to reinvent yourself, armed with your experience from the past about what you want out of relationships and out of yourself.

In this day and age, we're constantly traveling, moving, switching jobs: the average new graduate today will have *seven* jobs by the time they are thirty years old! Which makes it all the more rare and special to have one of those "forever friends." The award for Longest Friendship (outside of family) in my own life goes to one Shari Flowers—previously Shari Miller when we met at sleepaway camp at age eleven.

Boy, does Shari know me. She's seen the good, the bad, the wonderful, and the hideous. She was by my side for my first kiss (not literally). She's been punished alongside me (early bedtime for a week!) for being a bit . . . let's just say *creative*. She and I developed our own secret code for note passing. And in high school, she traveled with me for a month to Costa Rica, camping out on the floor of the rain forest. Years later, we met the men we wound up marrying within one week of one another, served as maid of honor in each other's weddings—only a year apart—and had sons within a month of each other. Shari is now a successful doctor in New Jersey. We see each other often and were texting just a few minutes before I sat down to write this. #HiShari! I feel lucky to have someone like Shari in my life, who's known me through it all and still, somehow, managed not to run away screaming.

PICK TWO TO CREATE ONE

Friends that sweat together, stay together. If you're having trouble repeatedly prioritizing friends or fitness, try combining the two and signing up for a fitness class with a friend, setting your next catch-up as a walk instead of over drinks, or enrolling in a fun run.

On the topic of making fitness fun with friends, I connected with Zara Martirosyan, Founder & CEO of inKin, a social fitness platform that helps people to become more active through friendly social fitness competitions. "Health is humankind's most crucial and valuable asset," Zara told me. "However, for the vast majority of people starting a healthy journey, it is much harder than it sounds. People often lack the motivation or simply don't know how and where to begin. Our goal is to educate them, aggregate their data from various fitness devices and apps, and help them to get active through socializing with their family, friends, and coworkers, through friendly competitions, gamification, and rewards. We knew it was working when one of us lost over thirty kilos [sixty-six pounds] in one year since working on the project."

inKin's mission is that fun social fitness challenges can help people change their behavior and pay attention to their well-being: while taking part in online fitness contests with others, they develop a habit of tracking such important vitals as the level of their daily activity, nutrition, and sleep.

If your big focus right now is on fitness, and you find yourself needing accountability, or desiring more time with friends, try combining the two in a fun and motivating way. Your current friends will thank you and you might make some great new friends out of the journey!

Sometimes, even if you want to be lopsided toward friends, you just have to admit when a friendship is toxic. Breaking up with a friend is an incredibly difficult thing to do. But if someone is having a negative effect on your life, you need to cut your losses and move along. We all have friends who turn out to be situational or who we grow apart from. Sometimes it can be quite painful to admit when a friendship has turned sour and needs to be ended. We struggle to hang on, we make excuses for bad behavior, we get nostalgic for old times together. But sometimes the best and strongest thing you can do is to admit you've grown apart in such drastically different ways that it's time to close the chapter on the friendship and love one another from a distance so that everyone can move on.

Some people love working with their close friends and gravitate toward their closest relationships in their business endeavors. Some people avoid it like the plague and will tell you that their best advice is to never, EVER go into business with a best friend. I've somehow managed to stay somewhere in the middle. I've invested money into good friends' companies, but I always make sure going in that it's a dollar amount that won't upset me if I lose it all. (That's a good investment principle in general when investing in high-risk, very speculative, early-stage start-ups—whether started by friends or not!) I've worked closely alongside great friends, but typically it's the case that we were more like friendly acquaintances when we started working together and then grew to be close the more time we spent together. I've also tried to ensure that when working with friends, those people have complementary—rather than overlapping—skill sets. As humans, we gravitate toward people who are similar to us, which can be comforting when starting something unpredictable like a new business or a big project. But too much similarity can be detrimental if two people have the exact same skill set and wind up stepping on each other's toes rather than balancing out each other's strengths and weaknesses.

At a Forbes and Capital One Spark Forum, Heidi Messer, founder of Collective[i], said, "In many ways, a business partnership is similar to a marriage. At minimum, you need absolute trust in your partner." I have had one particular instance in which taking on a project with a close friend had a detrimental effect on our friendship. I had been living in Silicon Valley for about a year and I think I had a total of about ten thousand dollars in my bank account, which was more than I had ever had, but I wasn't exactly rolling in it. However, I think a lot of people assumed that I was, because wherever you looked, Facebook was in the news with lots and lots and lots of zeroes being thrown around in the valuation of the company.

It was around that time a friend and I decided to embark on a small outside project together. We scoped out a plan, a schedule, a budget. In the beginning, it was awesome. It was super fun to be able to dive into a project with a close friend, spend lots of time together, and pool our creative energy. However, strain started to show every time expenses came due that we had previously agreed on together, when she would start crying poverty, and all the expenses wound up falling on me. That ten thousand dollars in my bank account was depleted very quickly, which affected some of my plans to travel that holiday season. And then, near the end of the project, that same friend presented me with a "revised partnership agreement" stating that she should own

75 percent of the project, rather than the 50/50 split we had previously agreed upon, because she claimed she was the one who had originally come up with the idea.

Well, I might have been naïve, but I certainly wasn't a doormat. We had a huge blow-up argument and to this day, our friendship has never quite recovered. I think if she had been honest with me early on about her finances or her ability to contribute, and her desired goals, we could have avoided a lot of the drama and heartache. Luckily, it wasn't a project that was Mission Critical for either of our careers or lives, it was just a small side hustle, but it was a lesson, learned relatively cheaply, about the risks that can happen when you go into business with a close friend.

But by all means, my experience doesn't mean you shouldn't do it! Lots of people are able to work closely alongside close friends or family members and can compartmentalize enough to make it all work. Starting a business can be lonely, and it's really a wonderful thing to have a business partner who you can lean on and confide in when the going gets rough. Just understand the risks going in, and try to negotiate the worst-case scenarios before you start. Getting ahead of conflict is the best way to ensure that both your business and your friendship come out alive!

Irene S. Levine, our Pick Three Friends Expert, is a professor of psychiatry at the New York University School of Medicine. Irene says, "People differ in terms of the number of friendships they need and the nature of the friendships they prefer. Depending on temperament and personality, some people like to have many loose social ties; others prefer a smaller number of more intimate/intense friendships. Our need for friends also changes across our life span, influenced by life circumstances and available free time."

As a woman and a psychologist, Irene has always had an interest in female friendships as well as a natural curiosity about how her friendships compared to those of other people she knew. She wondered why some friendships stuck while others seemed to slip away. Over the years, even relationships with best friends sometimes turn out to be fleeting.

When Overlook Press approached Irene to write a book about female friendships, it gave her the impetus to dig into the literature and speak to women of all ages about their experiences. She created an online survey that informed her book *Best Friends Forever: Surviving a Breakup with Your Best Friend*. What she found was that friendships are extremely important relationships, especially to women. "They help shape our identities and define the persons we become. They're nothing short of being life-enhancing!"

But Irene also found downsides to friendships. The loss of a friendship can feel like a personal failure, because in order to get close to another person, we suspend the possibility that the friendship will ever end. "Women are often judged by their ability to make and keep friends. Losing a close friend, particularly if the breakup is one-sided, hits hard. It feels like a failure and can be as painful as being jilted by a lover, getting divorced, or losing a spouse. Some friendships are stronger than blood relationships with relatives."

Irene says the cultural taboos against ending friendships are so strong that women are reluctant to end these relationships, even ones that are no longer mutually rewarding. And often a sizable number of people feel lonely and don't have a single friend they feel they can count on for support (for instance, to drive them to a medical appointment or to confide in about a problem with a child).

When it comes to the science behind friendships, Irene says that although the precise biological mechanisms still aren't clear, a number of studies have linked friendship and social supports to improved health and emotional outcomes, such as decreased risk for coronary artery disease, obesity, diabetes, high blood pressure, depression, and improved longevity.

And as for social media, it can enhance our ability to make friends and to nurture existing friendships. It makes it easy to communicate with friends across the country or across the globe asynchronously. However, it's easy for misunderstandings to occur when people can't see each other's expressions, body language, and so on.

BFFS FOR LIFE—LITERALLY!

"True friendship means showing up. Putting your tech aside and using your legs. It's so easy to send an e-mail or shoot a text. It's much harder to show up at the door when you haven't been invited." —AMY SILVERSTEIN, AUTHOR

Amy Silverstein is the author of *My Glory Was I Had Such Friends,* a memoir about nine friends she credits with saving her life when she was waiting for her *second* heart transplant at age fifty. And, if this story isn't inspiring enough, just two days after publication of her memoir, J. J. Abrams, of *Star Wars* and *Westworld* fame, acquired the rights to the book to develop as a limited series.

Amy had her first heart transplant at twenty-five. She had found out she was in heart failure, with a ten-year life expectancy, but she was determined not to have that be true. After twenty-six healthy years post-transplant, which is rare for hearts, Amy found herself needing a second heart and had to travel to L.A. for the procedure. After she moved, her close girlfriends decided that they weren't going to let her be alone, so they created a spreadsheet where they could all sign up for shifts, ensuring that someone would always be next to her the entire time. "People can rise up, especially when it's to save someone's life."

Amy wrote *My Glory* because she knew she had to write something about the miracle of her friends' showing up for her. The book delved into the changes in friendships between ages twenty-five and fifty, and how maturity helps you learn how to nurture and show up for each other. "When you're twenty-five, you're not the same kind of friend you are at fifty."

My Glory focuses on what each one of these women brought to Amy during her second transplant. They were all living different lives but were able to all rally around a central goal and make sacrifices in their own lives to help. Some of the friends knew one another beforehand and some did not. Nonetheless, they all began to develop a unique friendship as a group, and would e-mail one another about what to bring, when to come, and what they could do to ease Amy's fears. "I think my friends surprised themselves. There was something about it, a pay-it-forward sort of thing."

Amy has friends she's known most of her life and new ones that she's recently cultivated into close friendships. She knows her oldest friend from the second grade, two she knows from law school, two she met through her husband;

these friends and more all came to watch over her as she waited for her second heart transplant. The newest friend, more of a situational acquaintance prior to her surgery, came every single day while Amy was in the hospital, for two and a half months!

Amy said that when she first got the news that she would have to go out to L.A. on her own, she felt defeated, like she was going to die in L.A., lonely, scared, and abandoned while she waited for her new heart. But her sadness eased quickly when her friends came to see her. "My friends kept me alive to receive that organ. I couldn't do it without them."

To Amy, being a good friend isn't something you're born with. She wasn't a super friend at twenty-five. But she says by middle age people usually acquire the tools to show up in a more meaningful and authentic capacity. "It's easier to be a friend through an e-mail or text. But it feels great when you give someone a real hug."

If you've had an experience in your life where you unexpectedly found yourself leaning on your friends for support, I'm sure you thanked your lucky stars for the time you had invested into those friendships in the past, so you could call upon those people when you really needed them. Friendships can be funny, though. Sometimes, the people you expect to be there for you turn out to be quite disappointing. And sometimes it's the people you never expected who truly step up to the plate and go above and beyond.

Luckily, many of us are part of school, religious, or community organizations that can step in to help out for those of us who need a boost. It's easy to keep picking other things in our life to prioritize, and to keep saying, "I don't have time for friends right now, I'm too busy, I'm exhausted." But I keep thinking about that situation in the back of my mind—if

something big happened to me, have I put enough effort
into my friendships that my friends would be there for me?
Friends are like a savings account. If you've been a good
friend without expecting something immediate in return, if
you've risen to the occasion when your friends needed you,
then you've invested wisely. Because you truly never know,
as Amy found out, when those very same people might step
up and save your life

The plight of making new friends still plagues people today. Irene Levine says, "When we're children, it's easy to go up to someone in the playground or park and say, 'Can I play with you?' or 'Will you be my friend?' As we get older, we become more self-conscious about making new friends. People often succumb to the misperception that everyone already has all their friends—but nothing could be further from the truth. Friendships are often transient, changing with the circumstances of our lives as we graduate, move, marry, have children, change careers, divorce, become widows, and so on. Many people are looking for new friends."

Some friendships are hindered by geography and discrepant lifestyles, Irene explains. But if the friendship is inherently strong and important to both parties, people need to actively cultivate it by scheduling time to see each other and keeping in touch by phone, social media, or texting. "If someone begins to feel stressed at work and finds that they aren't performing optimally, it may be that they are spending too much time on social pursuits. Spending too much time with friends might also result in tensions in the family, e.g., neglecting responsibilities to children or a spouse."

On the flip side, if someone feels lonely and has no one to share their disappointments and successes, it might suggest that they should spend more time nurturing friendships. Irene notes, "People often think that spending time with friends is self-indulgent and discretionary. But the truth is that having strong friendships makes us better spouses, parents, and workers."

Friendship experts say there are no rules of the road for navigating friendships. Sometimes, it's even hard to know when a friendship starts and when it ends. It can be very difficult to know if someone is actually a true friend who will be there for you when push comes to shove, or if someone is just a situational friend who will run as soon as the road gets messy.

ASKING FRIENDS FOR MONEY (WITHOUT GETTING WEIRD)

Whether you're raising money for a charity fund-raiser, trying to fund a new project, or having a hard time making ends meet, asking friends for money can feel awkward and uneasy. Here are a few things to think about:

WILL IT AFFECT YOUR FRIENDSHIP? Does money add an unnecessary power imbalance into your friendship? Make sure you know the answer before proceeding.

HOW YOU ASK IS KEY. You never want to surprise someone or catch them off guard. Make sure you provide adequate details about how much you need and how you'll use the money. Appearing thoughtful with a plan always improves your odds of agreement. Always ask one-on-one, never in front of a group, and don't pressure for an answer on the spot. Think about how you would feel if the situation was reversed and give your friend ample time to think it over.

ARE THERE OTHER WAYS TO BE HELPFUL ASIDE FROM MONEY? If you think it might make things too weird, maybe there are other ways your friend can lend a hand: Making introductions to people, lending time, and giving expertise are all as valuable.

PUT IT IN WRITING. Create a hard copy contract you both sign. Keep a record of the investment and, if applicable, a repayment schedule. Doing a "handshake agreement" without putting anything in writing is the surest way to guarantee your friendship will not survive if things go south.

ASK FOR THE RIGHT AMOUNT. Figure out how much you really need. You typically get one chance with friends. Ask for enough so that you don't have to come back with outstretched hands for more, but not so much that the ask sounds outrageous.

FRIENDS SUPERHERO

Someone who needs to rethink their friend circle, and how to prioritize friends in order to support a loved one or themself.

"I was not involved and interested in the same lifestyles anymore. This helped my recovery by showing me I didn't have to manufacture everything in my life."

—HELEN, RECOVERY ADVOCATE

Helen has been a member of Alcoholics Anonymous for eight years—a decision about which she thinks many of her friends feigned happiness. "I felt sad because I thought it was a positive decision and direction, but I could see that behind the smiles was something else. Some thought I was being drastic, but I think most people felt some level of self-consciousness about their own relationship with substances. After all, I wasn't befriending people who had two and went home."

Helen had to stop going to bars and places where alcohol was served while she was in recovery, but she didn't do that right away. Her pride and ego told her she could spend time in the places she did before without having any cravings, but her thinking, she says, was quite foolish. "AA is a built-in habit makeover, really. Instead of a bar, you go to a meeting. You make friends there that you see over and over (the ones who stay) the way you saw the same people at the regular bars you frequented."

Since her recovery lifestyle is geared more toward spirituality, Helen relished the honesty and vulnerability that was present in her new way of life that many of her nonsober friends weren't interested in engaging in. "Many people were honored and touched to receive amends and even surprised I was making any."

There were people Helen had to part with who were strictly party friends. "They seemed to slip away easily. This helped my recovery by showing me I didn't have to manufacture everything in my life. I began allowing things to happen and unfold more organically. Not overnight, of course, but I learned I didn't have to do anything but stay sober."

And now Helen has a new group of friends to trust and rely on, friends who hold her accountable to her own BS. "The rigorous honesty they exhibit in their lives is so inspiring and healing to me. I see them stay sober through everything that could possibly happen to a human and cope with it soberly."

CAUTION: ALL LIVES LOOK MORE FUN ONLINE!

Never EVER compare yourself to someone else's Instagram page. Filters and Photoshop can do wonders, but real life cannot be edited. Of course, people are going to post the one moment where they're smiling, having fun, and looking glamorous. Enjoy posts and photos for what they really are: Nothing.

BE MINDFUL ABOUT YOUR TIME ON SOCIAL MEDIA. The entire purpose of social media is to make you feel closer to the people and things you care about. If it's not making you happy, think about how you can use sites in a more mindful way.

REMEMBER THAT EVERYONE IS DEALING WITH STUFF. I recently called a friend whose life looked pretty darn perfect online. When we got on the phone I told her how happy I was for her. To which she replied, "I recently got laid off last week and I'm super depressed." No matter what you think, everyone is fighting their own battle.

PEOPLE PROBABLY THINK YOUR LIFE IS AMAZING, TOO. If you're feeling down about the exciting lives of others, imagine what they must be feeling about yours! You have an opportunity to keep your posts authentic and represent what you're actually going through—the good and the bad. Don't be afraid to share moments of vulnerability. You'll find that many people will be able to relate.

As for how Helen chooses her friends now, she looks for conscious and aware people to befriend. "I prefer persons who do not depend on substances. I find the connection takes more work and effort than I'd like to put in, given that friendships and relationships already take work."

The best part of Helen's new group of friends is that there's an automatic code of understanding that they can be honest and vulnerable because they know that is the core of healing. The sharing and connection that can be lost in the everyday world is given to those in AA for free on a daily basis if they choose to partake.

But not every sober person does a new friend make. Helen says it really depends on the person. Sometimes it's harder because some people are not comfortable with just saying what is really going on with themselves. Since Helen does not want to have surface friendships, she prefers to find people who naturally understand the importance of depending on other humans for connection. "I learn a lot from them."

I am a naturally introverted person, so showing up by myself at an event where I don't know anybody can be quite terrifying! As a lover of the arts and opera, I go to a lot of events to explore what it means to be a patron of the arts. I don't want to generalize, but let's just say that oftentimes at these events, you could double my age and I'd still be the youngest person in the room . . . and everyone seems to know one another already since they've all been patrons of the arts in New York City together for some time now. At one particular event, I was feeling alone and unlike everyone, and it seemed like everyone else was there with a date or a group, just not so approachable to speak with. I'd go over to people to say hi and they would just not engage, or look at me like they should hand me their coat or order a drink or something. I started texting my husband, my coworkers, *anyone I knew* to see if anyone was available at the last minute to come join me. If only I had known about Scott Rosenbaum's start-up!

FRIENDS MONETIZER

Someone who starts a business around helping other people pick Friends.

> *"There's a social stigma of being alone, and before RentAFriend, there were no other options for hiring a nonsexual platonic escort."*
>
> **—SCOTT ROSENBAUM, CREATOR OF RENTAFRIEND.COM**

RentAFriend.com—yup, you read that correctly—is a company dedicated to buying your way into a platonic friendship. Scott Rosenbaum started RentAFriend back in October 2009 in Stewartsville, New Jersey. The idea derived from the increasing popularity of successful rent-a-friend companies already established in Japan. Scott had a lightbulb moment to bring that same model to the Western world.

RentAFriend is for people who want to see a movie or try a new restaurant, or even have tickets for a sporting event or concert but don't want to go alone. The ideal customer, says Scott, is someone who is happy, positive, and open-minded. A lot of professionals use the RAF Web site, such as business owners, doctors, and lawyers. People may have a work event and want to bring someone. People may be traveling to a new city and want someone from the area they can hire to show them around. Some people don't want to go to a bar or restaurant by themselves, so they will hire a friend to go out to eat or have a drink with.

Scott thinks it's hard for people to make friends nowadays because everyone is extremely busy. The economy isn't the best, and people are working longer hours, so they don't have time to socialize as much as they used to. "I know I'm guilty of it."

There's a social stigma for people to be in a relationship, Scott says. "I'm seeing that lots of my friends are still single. I recently came upon a statistic that people are staying single longer. But just a few generations back, people were getting married in their late teens and early twenties." People are expected to have their lives organized. A good job, a significant other, a house, and so on. "But it's not easy to get all of those things, so it's common for people to hire a friend as a plus-one date just so they look like they have life figured out."

When RentAFriend first opened, there was quite a bit of public backlash. "People accused me of taking advantage of lonely people, but that is certainly not the case. In fact, a majority of the members (people paying to hire friends) have plenty of real friends, and some are even in relationships. It's just possible they are in a unique circumstance where they need a platonic plus-one, and we are the site that caters to that."

While I'll admit that I have never rented a friend before (though I have traveled for business with colleagues who went on dating sites while in other cities just to meet someone who would take them around the city on a free day, specifically stating that they were not looking for something romantic), there's definitely something to be said about our culture in which we are all closer to "friends" (digitally speaking), but further from "friendship."

USING TECH TO MAKE FRIENDS

Technology has helped make meeting new friends easier, with a slew of apps to help break the ice. In Japan, a new app called **Tipsys** is aimed at helping Japanese women in need of friends. Tipsys is for female platonic friendships only and allows women to search locations, hobbies—even drink preferences. The only thing forbidden on the app is fishing for dates, so anyone who uses the app for romance will have their account deleted.

In the U.S., dating apps Bumble and Tinder have launched **Bumble BFF** and **Tinder Social** for users to find platonic friends. **Hey! VINA**, is a friendship-making app just for women, and since two is a date and three is a party, **Me3** helps you meet new people who share your interests, goals, and personality traits without swiping or ghosting. Users of Me3 are asked a series of game-show-like questions about personality, lifestyle, and beliefs, then matched into different tribes.

If you're in search of new friends, check out these other friendship-based apps:

MEETUP: Whether it's wine lovers or hiking fanatics, different meet-ups are available in thousands of cities around the world.

NEXTDOOR: Exchange community information and get local recommendations from the people right next to you: your neighbors.

PEANUT: A community of mothers who arrange in-person meet-ups and playdates.

SKOUT: Meet new people even if you're just visiting the area. Ideal for those who travel regularly.

NEARIFY: Alerts you to events that are happening near you. See what events people are attending and get personal recommendations to make it easy to find something to do any day of the week.

MEET MY DOG: See what dogs are in your area, chat with the owners, and set up doggie dates.

I aspire to choose Friends in my Pick Three more often. I am grateful for the friends I have in my life who accompany me to talks I give or to theater shows that I have to see as a Tony voter, because they know that's pretty much my only free time for friends. Yet I also know I'm in a phase of my life where having young children and a career that requires me to be on the road so much makes social engagements significantly less of a priority than I'd like. I'd like to think, however, that when push comes to shove and my friends need me, I'm always there for them, like Amy's friends who quite literally saved her life. Or the new friends Helen seeks out to help in her quest for a healthier life. I hope in the long run I'll be able to pick Friends more often and life will balance out. Maybe Julie or Susan can give me some tips—then again, I can always rent some friends—though my real ones are pretty great. That's the beauty of the Pick Three mantra—we're playing the long game, folks!

In the meantime, if you're reading this and have sent me a text, e-mail, Facebook message, or anything that I haven't responded to lately, just know that I see it, and I'm doing my best. It might take ten years, but I'm not giving up on friends! So, friends, please don't give up on me, either!

3

PICKING
YOUR THREE

I LOVE NUMBERS—I'm a total data nerd—so I took the liberty of calculating the total number of different Pick Three combinations you could choose. I came up with dozens, right? Hundreds?? Try ten. That's right, there are only ten possible Pick Three combos. Which means it's totally attainable to try them all! Take 'em all for a spin and see what fits best!

HERE ARE THE PICK THREE BIG TEN IN ALL THEIR GLORY:

WORK. SLEEP. FITNESS.

WORK. SLEEP. FAMILY.

WORK. SLEEP. FRIENDS.

WORK. FITNESS. FAMILY.

WORK. FITNESS. FRIENDS.

WORK. FAMILY. FRIENDS.

SLEEP. FITNESS. FAMILY.

SLEEP. FITNESS. FRIENDS.

SLEEP. FAMILY. FRIENDS.

FITNESS. FAMILY. FRIENDS.

When you break it down this way, Pick Three seems even more doable and less scary!

Remember, if you tried to pick all five every day, you'd burn out after a few days (which is maybe why you've picked up this book). The stress of striving for perfect balance may have even driven you to drink, shop, send emotional texts, or eat an entire chocolate cake (not that I'm speaking from experience or anything). I'm sorry to break it to you, I know you're a very capable human being, but most humans just sort of suck at multitasking. Don't believe me? Well, there's a ton of science to back that up.

The *Harvard Business Review* found that people are happier when they multitask over a longer amount of time, rather than in short bursts. In an experiment, students were asked to do a series of activities with different types of candy. One group performed a variety of tasks like evaluate the taste of gummy bears, name jelly beans, and organize M&M's by color, while the other group performed only one task on one candy. All participants had fifteen minutes to work on the tasks, then they were measured to see how happy and productive they felt. Lo and behold, the students who spent fifteen minutes doing the same task felt more productive—and happier—than the students who spent the time on a variety of tasks.[26]

Even further, a study done on repetition and variety in a Japanese bank found that workers who switch between a variety of tasks in a short time period are less productive than workers who stick to a similar set of activities over that same period. Findings showed that switching between tasks consumes cognitive resources and takes up memory space, which, in turn, can make people feel more stressed and limits their ability to excel at the task at hand (sound familiar?). So increasing variety among the activities that fill these shorter time periods decreases happiness by making workers feel less productive.[27]

There are a gazillion other studies showing that happiness and multitasking have a direct inverse correlation to one another.

Which is why Pick Three—focusing on only three tasks in a twenty-four-hour period—works! When you set your brain to accomplish only a few items, not only are you more successful, but your emotional well-being improves, too!

Which brings me back to our Pick Three Big Ten. If you'd stick with Pick Three for even one month, you'd find that you could tackle each of these ten combos *three times!* Giving quality attention to each of the five buckets of life while helping maintain stress and happiness levels! I'd say it's worth a shot, no?

TURNING YOUR TO-DO LIST INTO A TA-DA LIST

There are few organizational tips I dislike more than the to-do list. Honestly, what is a to-do list, really, other than a written-out tally of how inadequate you are at a whole bunch of things you haven't done yet. Your tasks just stare you in the face until you're either shamed enough to take them on or you just say "screw it" and acknowledge that they'll just never get done!

Do you ever feel this way, too?

Some people completely disagree with me and love their to-do lists. They love the satisfaction of crossing off items and feeling that they've accomplished something. Those same people probably also have inbox zero, clean desks, and perfect bodies. But even they, too, can benefit from the wonders of Pick Three. (The jerks.)

I will never get to inbox zero, that's a reality I've had to face. Just like I'll never have a perfectly clean desk or find that matching sock. I've come to terms with both of these on the theory that messiness = creativity (at least that's what I tell myself to sleep better at night).

By picking three things each day, suddenly a daunting to-do list feels more like a "Ta-da! You did it!" list. Close the curtain and end the day with a bow. Cue thunderous applause. But if you want to make this a long-term thing, you'll need to hold yourself accountable. Which means you need to track your progress, which means a different sort of list—the Ta-Da List!

On pages 224 and 225, you'll find my basic weekly Pick Three chart.

After you've tracked your priorities for a week, see how the numbers add up and ask yourself:

HOW MANY TIMES DID YOU PICK EACH OF THE CATEGORIES?

WORK:

SLEEP:

FAMILY:

FITNESS:

FRIENDS:

ARE THERE ANY CATEGORIES THAT YOU PICKED FEWER THAN THREE TIMES?

IF SO, IS THAT NORMAL, OR WAS THIS WEEK UNUSUAL?

_____

**ARE THERE ANY CATEGORIES THAT YOU PICKED MORE
THAN FIVE TIMES?**

_____

**IF SO, IS THAT TYPICAL FOR YOU, OR DID SOMETHING
HAPPEN THIS WEEK THAT WAS AN OUTLIER?**

_____

**HOW DID YOUR GOALS FOR WHAT YOU WANTED TO ACHIEVE
DIFFER FROM WHAT ACTUALLY HAPPENED?**

_____

HOW WOULD YOU LIKE NEXT WEEK TO LOOK? THE SAME? DIFFERENT?

_____

HERE'S WHERE IT GETS FUN: You probably already know if you're a
Passionista, an Eliminator, a Superhero, a Renovator, or a Monetizer, but if you're in a bit of a self-discovery phase, take stock of
those around you to help see where you fit on the chart. Sometimes it can be easier to look outward than it is to look inward,
so try to identify a few other people in your life who are well
lopsided, then see who you most relate to.

PICK THREE SCORECARD

Track your priorities for a week (and ideally longer!) to see where you net out.

	WORK	SLEEP
MONDAY		
GOAL	x	
ACTUAL	x	x
TUESDAY		
GOAL		
ACTUAL		
WEDNESDAY		
GOAL		
ACTUAL		
THURSDAY		
GOAL		
ACTUAL		
FRIDAY		
GOAL		
ACTUAL		
SATURDAY		
GOAL		
ACTUAL		
SUNDAY		
GOAL		
ACTUAL		

FAMILY	FITNESS	FRIENDS
X	X	
	X	X

NAME SOMEONE FROM YOUR LIFE WHO IS A:

Work

Passionista:

How are they able to prioritize work so often? What support systems do they have in place to help them?

_____

_____

_____

_____

_____

Eliminator :

Is this by choice or by circumstance? How do they spend their time?

_____

_____

_____

_____

_____

Superhero:

How did a loved one's needs impact their career goals?

_____

_____

_____

_____

_____

Renovator:
_____

What was their career "a-ha" or wake-up moment that made them realize they needed to change?

_____

_____

_____

_____

_____

Monetizer:
_____

How have they turned their passion for the workplace into a business?

_____

_____

_____

_____

Sleep

Passionista:
_____

How are they able to get enough sleep?

_____

_____

_____

Eliminator:
_____

How are they able to function when eliminating sleep?

_____

_____

_____

_____

Superhero:

Who is responsible for their lack of sleep? Is their situation permanent or temporary?

_____

_____

_____

_____

_____

_____

Renovator:

What was their exhaustion wake-up call moment?

_____

_____

_____

_____

_____

_____

Monetizer:

How have they turned sleep into a business?

_____

_____

_____

_____

_____

Family

Passionista:

How are they able to prioritize family so often?

_____

_____

_____

_____

_____

Eliminator:

Who fills the family space for them?

_____

_____

_____

_____

Superhero:

How did they have to change their family plans to accommodate a loved one?

_____

_____

_____

_____

Renovator:

What family roadblock did they hit? How did they rebuild?

_____

_____

_____

_____

Monetizer:

How have they turned family into a business?

_____
_____
_____
_____

Fitness

Passionista:

How are they able to prioritize fitness so often?

_____
_____
_____
_____

Eliminator:

Are they living a healthy lifestyle?

_____
_____
_____
_____

Superhero:

How did a loved one's needs impact their fitness goals?

_____
_____
_____
_____

Renovator:

What fitness challenges have they overcome? How did they do it?

_____

_____

_____

_____

_____

Monetizer:

How have they turned fitness into a business?

_____

_____

_____

_____

_____

Friends

Passionista:

How are they able to make these relationships so meaningful?

_____

_____

_____

_____

_____

_____

Eliminator:

Who fills the friends role for them?

_____

_____

_____

_____

Superhero:

How has a loved one's needs affected their friendships?

_____

_____

_____

_____

Renovator:

What friendship challenges have they had to overcome? How did they do it?

_____

_____

_____

_____

Monetizer:

How have they turned friends into a business?

_____

_____

_____

_____

_____

Now, who are you? Each of these questions can be answered for any of the areas—Work, Sleep, Family, Fitness, or Friends—so start with one for now to discover why and how you have come to prioritize certain areas in your own life. But remember, just because you're one thing today, doesn't mean you can't be something totally different tomorrow! So make sure you're constantly coming back to these and reassessing where you are with your goals.

YOUR PASSIONISTA SCORE:

Is there an area that you consistently pick more than five times each week?

_____

_____

_____

_____

_____

_____

_____

Are you lopsided in this area because you *want* to be, not because you *have* to be?

_____

_____

_____

_____

_____

_____

_____

_____

Would your family and friends agree with your assessment?

_____

_____

_____

_____

_____

_____

Do you get joy, pride, and/or a sense of fulfillment from this area?

_____

_____

_____

_____

_____

_____

_____

YOUR RENOVATOR SCORE:

Is there an area that you keep picking, but acknowledge that you are struggling with?

_____

_____

_____

_____

_____

_____

Have you recently gone through a major life change that has forced you to prioritize an area you hadn't prioritized before?

_____

_____

_____

_____

_____

_____

_____

_____

Do your priorities look a lot different today than a few months ago? Days ago?

_____

_____

_____

_____

_____

_____

_____

Would you say that you have had to adjust your goals significantly in this area over time?

_____

_____

_____

_____

_____

_____

_____

_____

YOUR SUPERHERO SCORE:

Do you have an area you consistently pick because of a loved one or life event?

_____

_____

_____

_____

_____

_____

_____

Is this area different than what you likely would pick if you were totally free to choose for yourself?

_____

_____

_____

_____

_____

_____

_____

_____

Do you sometimes feel that this category is picking you, instead of you picking it?

_____

_____

_____

_____

_____

_____

_____

Have you surprised yourself with your ability to be strong in this area, or prioritized it in a new way?

_____

_____

_____

_____

_____

_____

YOUR ELIMINATOR SCORE:

Do you have an area you consistently pick fewer than three times per week?

_____

_____

_____

_____

_____

_____

_____

Do you eliminate this area by choice?

_____

_____

_____

_____

_____

_____

_____

Do you feel that by eliminating this area, you have more time to focus on other areas of your life?

_____

_____

_____

_____

_____

_____

Do you often find it easier to make decisions by process of elimination, knowing what not to do, rather than what to do?

_____

_____

_____

_____

_____

_____

_____

YOUR MONETIZER SCORE:

Do you consistently prioritize helping other people lead better, happier, easier lives?

_____

_____

_____

_____

_____

_____

_____

Do you make money from the work you do to help other people become Passionistas in any of the five areas?

_____

_____

_____

_____

_____

_____

Do you get a sense of fulfillment from helping others pick this area?

_____

_____

_____

_____

_____

_____

_____

Are customers willing to buy into this vision? Are you providing a service people are willing to pay for to help prioritize a certain area in their life?

_____

_____

_____

_____

_____

_____

_____

If you answered "yes" to all or most of the four questions in any of these categories, congrats! Some people overwhelmingly identify with one persona, others are a combination of a few. Either way, now you know who you are (for today, at least). That's the beauty of Pick Three, it can all change tomorrow. And the day after that. Every single day you get to reinvent yourself while getting sh*t done! Like a boss!

It's totally okay if you feel like your Pick Three choices and who you are vary significantly. Maybe you're a "weekend Passionista" or a "summer Monetizer" or a "Monday Eliminator." There are so many different things you can be, and so many different life stages that will influence your Pick Three. Gosh, it would be so boring (and unhealthy) to pick the same three things every single day for your entire life. Which is why it's key to repeat these activities and ask yourself these questions on a regular basis, to make sure you understand how your goals and priorities are changing.

WHO AM I?

	WORK	SLEEP	FAMILY	FITNESS	FRIENDS
PASSIONISTA					
RENOVATOR					
SUPERHERO					
ELIMINATOR					
MONETIZER					

I'm sure a load of you ticked off Sleep Passionista, which is great! As long as you're a Sleep Passionista WHO SLEEPS. Be brutally honest with yourself as you're choosing your own Pick Three. You're not helping anybody by claiming to be something you aren't. Pinpointing your areas of strength and weaknesses, and identifying where you are too lopsided or not lopsided enough, is the most important takeaway here. We are all a work in process. So no more guilt! No more pretending to be somebody you're not! The point of Pick Three is to allow you to be well lopsided in a way that fits into your lifestyle and is authentically you.

If, like Ellen Dworsky, you're a Family Eliminator, it might not be as important to you to pick Family. And that's okay. But Eliminators in one area need to make sure their other needs are being met, like time with friends, fitness levels, etc. And even if you don't have children of your own, you likely have other family members who are waiting for a call or text. This book is not called Pick One, for a reason.

To be proud of all you can accomplish—especially nowadays, with the high-pressure, high-tech, high-maintenance lifestyle many people in business choose to embrace—there has to be a little bit of sacrifice. But it doesn't have to come from a place of pain or struggle. Pick Three allows you to choose when and why you want to lean toward one thing and away from another.

This also feels like a good time to say that your five categories might be different than mine. I picked Work, Sleep, Family, Fitness, and Friends because I can see how everything important in my life easily fits into one of those buckets. The Pick Three lifestyle is more about giving yourself permission to be focused and lopsided—to clear space for you to achieve your dreams—than it is to be locked down to a specific five buckets. Some people might make Travel a key category. Others might say Social Good is of paramount importance to them. Others might say Mental Health is a priority above all else. Even if your five are: Netflix. School. Tacos. Dating. Yoga. You still can't do everything well every single day, no matter what your own personal Pick Three categories are.

CHALLENGE:

CAN YOU TRY ONE OF THESE TIPS EVERY WEEK?

Since we can only Pick Three every day, we're all naturally going to have areas that we do well at prioritizing and other areas that we, maybe—*ahem*—need to do a bit better. Luckily, the experts I spoke to have given us some great wisdom to kick-start our efforts to pick some of our "forgotten" categories a bit more.

WILL YOU JOIN ME IN TAKING ON THE CHALLENGE OF TRYING OUT ONE OF THESE NEW TIPS EACH WEEK?

Try MaryJo Fitzgerald's recommendation of building short rest times into your workday. If needed, set calendar reminders to step away from your desk for 10 minutes for a quick stroll, a drink of water, or just a change of scenery. Our brains need rest time to perform at optimal levels.

Work

Even better, try out Ted Eytan's recommendation of having walking meetings instead of sitting in conference rooms or coffee shops.

Whether you are a Work Passionista, a Work Eliminator, or somewhere in between, take the advice of Melinda Arons and Karen Zuckerberg and make sure you have other outlets for your energy, like a hobby, a charity, a class, or a new skill that will look good on a future résumé!

Think about moments in your career that have felt like failures. Then ask yourself, "What would Reshma Saujani do?" Reframe failures in your mind as pivots on the path to success!

If you need help staying on track with your career goals or your "side hustle," follow Tina Yip's advice on how to hold yourself accountable, by setting 30-day goals or 100-day goals, and telling as many people about your end goal as possible.

Sleep Try Arianna Huffington's suggestion of "putting your phone to bed" in another room while you sleep. (Or, if you can't bear to be that far from your phone, try plugging it in on the other side of the room so you don't check it every 2 seconds.)

Take Hubspot's Brian Halligan's advice to have beanbag chairs available for 20–30-minute power naps during the day.

A TWO-MONTH TALLY

Welcome to your productivity scorecard. Tracking your Pick Three for a few weeks will give you a pretty clear sense of where your priorities lie, what you enjoy doing versus what you feel required to do, what makes you feel fulfilled, and which areas you're routinely neglecting.

	WORK	SLEEP
WEEK 1		
WEEK 2		
WEEK 3		
WEEK 4		
WEEK 5		
WEEK 6		
WEEK 7		
WEEK 8		

FAMILY	FITNESS	FRIENDS

Plan a vacation that centers around the theme of rest and relaxation. Whether it's a cruise on one of Lisa Lutoff-Perlo's ships, a spa retreat, or even just a staycation at home.

Take a tune from Jenni June and make sure hardcore exercise or big meals happen more than three hours before bedtime.

Family Set clear boundaries between family time and work time. Because of tech, work is with us 24/7. Nobody at work will set boundaries for you. You need to set those yourself—then stick to them!

If you're thinking of working with or for a family member like Ruth Zive or Brigitte Daniel, think hard about the pros and cons before you dive in, because there is always more at stake when family is involved.

If the family you were born into isn't providing a healthy relationship, or is too geographically far away, try seeking "family" through spirituality, community, or religion.

Remember that family decisions are your decisions. You don't have to explain yourself, defend your choices, or feel guilty for anything.

If you are a stay-at-home parent, find the joy in little things like Ramya Kumar does. Be silly and enjoy the opportunity to relive your childhood again.

Fitness

Making fitness a more social event is a great way to get started. Take a class, go for a walk with friends, exercise with your partner like Jenny Jurek does, or use tools like inKin to help others motivate you.

Follow fitness expert Tony Horton's advice and set a long-term goal, with daily microgoals to help you get there. The journey to weight loss, finishing a marathon, or getting healthy all begin and end with single steps.

Brian Patrick Murphy's ethos is that you need to find a community that makes fitness fun so you'll be more likely to consistently stick with it! Also, for optimal health and hotness, make your diet a major focus as well.

Remember that "fitness" encompasses many things related to health: mental fitness, emotional fitness, stress levels, addiction recovery, mindfulness. It's not only about pumping iron at the gym. So make sure not to neglect all the important areas of health and wellness.

Tim Bauer put it well when he said that all fitness goals need to have a "why" to keep you motivated. If that "why" is related to self-love, you're much more likely to stick with it long term.

Keep a journal of your fitness activity, or record it in an app, to keep yourself accountable.

Friends Susan McPherson recommends making sure that you have small check-ins with a few friends every day, even if it's just a text message to say hello.

If you're in a new city, new job, or new situation, technology can be a great help in making new friends and keeping you connected to your existing ones.

Be careful about taking on projects with friends. I'm not saying don't do it. Just make sure you think carefully and plan for what could happen if things don't go well.

Actively put yourself in situations to meet like-minded people, whether that's signing up for a class, attending a meetup, volunteering, joining an organization, or even just looking up from your phone for two minutes!

If a friendship has become toxic or simply run its course, end it. Appreciate the friendship for what it was in your life, and then end the chapter and turn the page. Life is too short to hold on to people who aren't supporting you and your goals.

Let me know how your progress is going by tagging me on Instagram or Twitter @randizuckerberg #pickthree.

Welcome to a new way of structuring your life—a life based on your decision, your choice, your Pick Three. I hope it serves you as well as it has me. And for that, enjoy my send-off haikus!

Balance? Not for me
I'd rather be lopsided
And go for my dreams

You can't have it all
At least not all in one day
Me? I just Pick Three

Whether I choose Work
Friends, Fitness, Sleep, Family
I always choose me

ACKNOWLEDGMENTS

I know I just spent an entire book telling you to Pick Three, but it's impossible for me to pick only three people to thank.

WORK: A huge thank you to the Dey Street team, the best team in publishing! A special thanks to Lisa Sharkey, my partner-in-crime, social media mastermind, and creative muse on three books now, and to Alieza Schvimer, my editor extraordinaire, for nudging me along in that special way editors nudge writers when she really wanted me to pick writing this book in my daily Pick Three. Thanks also go to: Lynn Grady, Anna Montague, Ben Steinberg, Kendra Newton, Heidi Richter, Serena Wang, Renata De Oliveira, and Mumtaz Mustafa.

SLEEP: Thank you to Andrew Blauner, my literary agent—I sleep better at night knowing that I have the most caring, intelligent agent in publishing on my side.

FAMILY: A world of gratitude to my husband Brent Tworetzky, who has now put up with me as a writing hermit for way more books than he ever bargained for. To my sons Asher and Simi who inspire me every single day. To my in-laws, Marla and Eron Tworetzky, for staying up all hours of the night to help me copy-edit this manuscript. And to my own mother, Karen Zuckerberg, for being so brave and authentic in allowing me to interview her for this book.

FITNESS: It was a bit of a sprint to interview more than forty people for this book in a time span of only a few weeks, but I am so grateful to all the incredible people who opened their hearts and their calendars to me, and were so willing to share their stories with honesty, authenticity, and openness. I laughed, I cried, I learned a ton. Thank you!

FRIENDS: I'm so very lucky to have colleagues who I also consider some of my dearest friends. I am grateful beyond words to Jim Augustine, Steve Anderson, Emma Pendry-Aber, Jesus Gonzalez, Aranza Martinez, and the entire team at JonesWorks PR, for being by my side through this entire process.

NATASHA: And because you deserve your own category, Natasha Lewin, thank you for being the best collaborator, researcher, and colleague a girl could dream of. From being writing buddies in a hotel lounge in Korea to our multihour FaceTime chats to edit interviews, there wouldn't be a book without you! Thank you!

NOTES

INTRODUCTION

1. Helliwell, John, Richard Layard, and Jeffrey Sachs, "World Happiness Report 2017." http://worldhappiness.report /wpcontent/uploads/sites/2/2017/03/HR17-Ch7.pdf

2. Hydzik, Allison, "Using lots of social media sites raises depression risk," University of Pittsburgh Brain Institute, February 1, 2018. http://www.braininstitute.pitt.edu/using -lots-social-media-sites-raises-depression-risk

3. "Instagram ranked worst for young people's mental health," Royal Society for Public Health, May 19, 2017. https:// www.rsph.org.uk/about-us/news/instagram-ranked-worst -for-young-people-s-mental-health.html

4. McCarriston, Gregory, "26% of Americans say a negative internet comment has ruined their day," YouGov, September 7, 2017. https://today.yougov.com /news/2017/09/07/26-americans-say-negative-internet -comment-has-rui/

WORK

5. "What is tall poppy syndrome?" Oxford Press. http://blog
   .oxforddictionaries.com/2017/06/tall-poppy-syndrome/
6. Deane OBE, Julie, "Self-Employment Review," February
   2016. https://www.hudsoncontract.co.uk/media/1165
   /selfemployment-review-jdeane.pdf
7. "Glassdoor Survey Finds Americans Forfeit Half of Their
   Earned Vacation/Paid Time Off," Glassdoor, May 24, 2017.
   https://www.glassdoor.com/press/glassdoor-survey-finds
   -americans-forfeit-earned-vacationpaid-time/
8. Hewlett, Sylvia Ann and Carolyn Buck Luce, "Off-Ramps
   and On-Ramps: Keeping Talented Women on the Road to
   Success," Harvard Business Review, March 2005. https://
   hbr.org/2005/03/off-ramps-and-on-ramps-keeping-talented
   -women-on-the-road-to-success
9. Fishman Cohen, Carol, "Honoring Return-to-Work Dads,"
   iRelaunch, February 1, 2018. https://www.irelaunch.com
   /blog-fathers-day
10. Eytan, Ted, "The Art of the Walking Meeting," TedEytan
    .com, January 10, 2008. https://www.tedeytan.com/2008
    /01/10/148

SLEEP

11. Geggel, Laura, "Watch Out: Daylight Saving Time May
    Cause Heart Attack Spike," LiveScience, March 7, 2015.
    https://www.livescience.com/50068-daylight-saving-time
    -heart-attacks.html
12. Potter, Lisa Marie and Nicholas Weiler, "Short Sleepers Are
    Four Times More Likely to Catch a Cold," University of
    California San Francisco, August 31, 2015. https://www

.ucsf.edu/news/2015/08/131411/short-sleepers-are-four
-times-more-likely-catch-cold

13. Nathaniel F. Watson, MD, et al., "Recommended Amount
of Sleep for a Healthy Adult: A Joint Consensus Statement
of the American Academy of Sleep Medicine and Sleep
Research Society," *Journal of Clinical Sleep Medicine*,
November 6, 2015. https://aasm.org/resources/pdf
/pressroom/adult-sleep-duration-consensus.pdf

14. Marco Hafner, et al., "Why sleep matters—the economic
costs of insufficient sleep," RAND Europe, November
2016. https://thesleepschool.org/RAND%20Sleep%20
report.pdf

15. "The Impact of School Start Times on Adolescent Health
and Academic Performance, schoolstarttime.org, February
1, 2018. https://schoolstarttime.org/early-school-start-times
/academic-performance/

16. Harmon, Katherine, "Rare Genetic Mutation Lets Some
People Function with Less Sleep," Scientific American,
August 13, 2009. https://www.scientificamerican.com
/article/genetic-mutation-sleep-less/

17. Feldman, Amy, "Dozens of Upstart Companies Are
Upending the $15-Billion Mattress Market," Forbes,
May 2, 2017. https://www.forbes.com/sites/amyfeldman
/2017/05/02/dozens-of-upstart-companies-are-upending
-the-15-billion-mattress-market/#5f472a617da3

18. Weiler Reynolds, Brie, "2017 Annual Survey Finds Workers
Are More Productive at Home, and More," FlexJobs,
August 21, 2017. https://www.flexjobs.com/blog/post
/productive-working-remotely-top-companies-hiring/

19. Howington, Jessica, "Survey: Changing Workplace Priorities of Millennials," FlexJobs, September 25, 2015. https://www.flexjobs.com/blog/post/survey-changing-workplace-priorities-millennials/

20. "1 in 3 adults don't get enough sleep," Center for Disease Control and Prevention, February 18, 2016. https://www.cdc.gov/media/releases/2016/p0215-enough-sleep.html.

21. Weiler Reynolds, Brie, "6 Ways Working Remotely Will Save You $4,600 Annually, or More," FlexJobs, February 1, 2017. https://www.flexjobs.com/blog/post/6-ways-working-remotely-will-save-you-money/

22. "Driving Tired," Discovery: Mythbusters. http://www.discovery.com/tv-shows/mythbusters/about-this-show/tired-vs-drunk-driving/

FAMILY

23. Rubin, Rita, "U.S. Dead Last Among Developed Countries When It Comes to Paid Maternity Leave," Forbes, April 6, 2016. https://www.forbes.com/sites/ritarubin/2016/04/06/united-states-lags-behind-all-other-developed-countries-when-it-comes-to-paid-maternity-leave/#3491954a8f15

24. "Reclaim Your Vacation," Alamo, February 1, 2018. https://www.alamo.com/en_US/car-rental/scenic-route/vacation-tales/vacation-shaming.html

25. Stephanie L. Brown, et al., "Providing Social Support May Be More Beneficial Than Receiving It," SAGE Journals, July 1, 2003. http://journals.sagepub.com/doi/abs/10.1111/1467-9280.14461

PART 3: PICKING YOUR THREE

26. Etkin, Jordan and Cassie Mogilner, "When Multitasking Makes You Happy and When It Doesn't," Harvard Business Review, February 26, 2015. https://hbr .org/2015/02/when-multitasking-makes-you-happy-and -when-it-doesnt

27. Staats, Bradley R. and Francesca Gino, "Specialization and Variety in Repetitive Tasks." http://public.kenan-flagler.unc .edu/Faculty/staatsb/focus.pdf

ABOUT THE AUTHOR

Randi Zuckerberg is an entrepreneur, author, tech media personality, and champion for women and girls in STEM. Randi is the creator and executive producer of *Dot.*, an animated television show about a tech-savvy girl named Dot, based on her children's picture book of the same name. Randi is also the founder of Sue's Tech Kitchen, an innovative tech-themed family dining experience, where you can enjoy 3D printed chocolate, robots making pancakes, and much more. Randi hosts a weekly business radio show, "Dot Complicated," on SiriusXM and is invited to speak about technology, entrepreneurship, and women in business all over the world. In her (barely) free time, she can be found at the theater. By far, her most rewarding and challenging job is Mom. Randi has a degree in psychology from Harvard University and lives in New York City with her husband and two sons.